MaryEllen's

BEST
of
helpful
Kitchen
hints

Mary Ellen's BEST of helpful Kitchen hints

by

MARY ELLEN PINKHAM

illustrations by
LYNN JOHNSTON

WARNER BOOKS

A Warner Communications Company

Note

To obtain the best results and to avoid damage, the author and the publisher recommend care and common sense in the use of the hints in this book.

THE BEST OF HELPFUL KITCHEN HINTS FOR

Introduction

Every day you face problems in the kitchen—and so does everyone else. The meringue on your favorite lemon pie suddenly begins to weep and sink. The cookies stick to the baking pan. You open a carton of eggs, and six of them are cracked. I figured you—and everyone else—needed a book that could help you handle such unpredictable disasters. A book like our first one, Mary Ellen's Best of Helpful Hints, but specially designed for kitchen use—a book full of hints that really work, that are easy and fun to look up when you need them most. This is it!

Many of the hints in this book are original, but many also come from you, the people from all over the country who responded to our first book by sharing their own suggestions. I've read and tested them, plus thousands of others, and have organized the very best of them into convenient categories for easy reference when you need a solution to a problem right away.

As you use this book you'll find that what works in the kitchen is often valuable in solving other dilemmas around the home, too. If you're like me, you've discovered that applying to new situations the simple techniques you use in the kitchen can help you in everything from cleaning to child-rearing; and I'm sure that in this collection of over a thousand ideas, you'll find plenty of new ways to save time, money, and trouble—and an expensive trip to the grocery store.

The Best of Helpful Kitchen Hints for
Cooking

In the Beginning

Recipes at the ready

- Keep a recipe card upright by placing it in the tines of a fork and putting the fork handle in a glass. Carry the glass with you from counter to range as you cook.
- Or use a small magnet to tack the recipe card to the refrigerator or exhaust-fan hood.
- Or hang a permanent clamp on the inside, or even the outside, of a cupboard door, just for this purpose.
- Or, if you keep your recipe cards in a card-file box, glue a cork to the top of the box. Cut a slot across the top of the cork and simply insert the card you need to use in an upright position.

You'll see right through this

- To keep a recipe book or card clean while you're cooking, place it under an upside-down glass pie plate. The curved bottom also magnifies the print.
- Protect recipe cards from drips by using see-through plastic-covered file cards or by taping plastic wrap over the front.
- Or apply a thin coat of clear nail polish.
- Or spray with hair spray.

Cookbook update

- When you find a better recipe than one in your cookbook, copy it onto a file card and tape it over the recipe in your book. This way, you can use the book's index to find your new, improved recipe.
- Another trick is gluing an envelope to the inside of the front cover to hold new recipe cards and newspaper clippings.

From the Soup

Puree and simple
- Before your extra mushrooms go bad, use your blender to puree them in a little liquid (water, beef, or chicken broth), pour into ice-cube trays, and freeze. Remove when solid and store in freezer in plastic bags. Great for soups, stews, or sauces.
- Keep putting all leftover vegetables in a container in your freezer. When you have a sufficient amount, blend and freeze in ice-cube trays. Just thaw amount needed. Good for adding additional flavor to frozen soups.
- When cooking a beef roast, save pan juice. Pour it into ice-cube trays and freeze. Wrap solid cubes in foil and store in freezer. You will have instant beef stock when needed.

No bones about it
- Beef stock will obtain a rich brown color if bones are first browned under broiler about six inches from heat. Then add bones to stock and proceed to cook.
- When preparing soups or broths, remember that the gelatin in the bones gives body to the liquids and that veal bones, if available, give soup the most body.
- Don't throw away steak, roast, or chicken bones. Wrap and freeze until needed for soup stock.
- Always start cooking bones and meat in cold, salted water.

I want to make this perfectly clear
- Adding two or three eggshells to your soup stock and simmering it for ten minutes will help clarify the broth.
- Or strain stock through clean nylon hose or coffee filter.

Smoother soup—no scorching, clumping, or curdling

- To prevent scorching when cooking soup in a large stock pot, elevate the pot above the flame by putting two or three bricks on the burner. The platform permits long-term simmering over low heat without worries of boil-overs.
- When making split-pea soup, add a slice of bread when you start cooking the liquid and peas together. This will keep the peas from going to the bottom and burning or sticking.
- To prevent curdling of the milk or cream in tomato soup, add the tomato soup to the milk rather than vice versa.
- Or first add a little flour to the milk and beat well.
- Add minced clams to chowder at the very last moment. Otherwise they become mushy and tasteless.

Skimming off the fat

- If time allows, the best method is to refrigerate the soup until the fat hardens on the top.
- Eliminate fat from soup and stew by dropping ice cubes into the pot. As you stir, the fat will cling to the cubes. Discard the cubes before they melt.
- Or wrap ice cubes in a piece of cheesecloth or paper towel and skim over the top.
- Lettuce leaves also absorb fat. Place a few in the pot and remove them with the fat that clings to them.

To the Salad

Freshenin' up

- To remove the core from a head of lettuce, hit the core end once against the counter top sharply. The core will then twist out. This method also prevents the unsightly brown spots that result from cutting into lettuce.
- Fit the bottom of a colander with a nylon net and use as a receptacle for salad ingredients. When batch is washed, take the net out by the edges, squeeze out the water, and you've got everything handy for the salad bowl.
- Put cut-up salad greens or cole slaw in a metal bowl and place in freezer for a few minutes. The greens will arrive on the table in perky condition.
- To prevent soggy salads, place an inverted saucer in the bottom of the salad bowl. The excess liquid drains off under the saucer and the salad stays fresh and crisp.
- Do not add salt to a lettuce salad until just before serving—salt wilts and toughens lettuce.

Dressin' up

- Add a tablespoon of boiling water to an envelope of your favorite salad-dressing mix, cover, and let cool. The flavor is released immediately. Add other ingredients as usual.
- Make creamy dressings by pouring oil slowly into other ingredients in a slow-running blender.

Shakin' up

- Combine all ingredients for an oil-and-vinegar dressing in a screw-top jar. Add an ice cube and shake. Discard the ice cube and your dressing will be extra smooth and well mixed.
- Then put salad greens in a plastic bag, add dressing, and shake.

Storin' up

- Lettuce will not rust so quickly if you line the bottom of the refrigerator's vegetable compartment with paper towels or napkins. The paper absorbs the excess moisture, keeping vegetables and fruits fresher for a longer period of time.
- Or put a few dry sponges in the vegetable compartment to absorb moisture.

Toppin' up

- Slice leftover hot-dog buns into sticks, butter them, sprinkle with garlic powder and Parmesan cheese, then toast them in oven. Crumble them over salads.
- For a richer-looking potato salad, add some yellow food coloring to the mixed ingredients.

Do's

- Do add a touch of garlic by rubbing a crushed clove of garlic over the inside of the salad bowl before adding salad ingredients.
- Do keep packages of blue or Roquefort cheese in freezer. The cheese will crumble perfectly if scraped with a paring knife, and will be ready to serve with salad dressing by dinnertime.
- To keep a wooden salad bowl from becoming sticky, wash and dry it thoroughly, then rub bowl well, inside and out, with a piece of waxed paper.
- Or rub the inside of a wooden bowl with a piece of walnut meat. This also removes scratches.

And a don't

- Don't use a painted plate for serving salad with vinegar dressing. Vinegar corrodes the paint on the plate.

Vim, Vigor, and Vegetables

Artichokes

- Wear rubber gloves when handling artichokes and you won't prick your fingers while snipping off the ends of the leaves with scissors and removing the choke.
- Don't cook artichokes in an aluminum or iron pot. They turn the pot gray.
- To prevent their discoloring, stand artichokes in cold water with a tablespoon of vinegar an hour before cooking or dip the trimmed base in lemon juice.
- Wrap artichokes, unwashed, in a damp towel and store in a plastic bag in the refrigerator. This will prevent wilting for up to five days.

Asparagus

- Open asparagus cans from the bottom to avoid breaking the tips.
- Use a clean coffee percolator to cook fresh asparagus. The asparagus stand upright this way—stalk side down—and the tips steam perfectly while the stems cook to a tender finish.
- To revive limp, uncooked asparagus, stand them upright in a small amount of ice water in a deep pot and cover with a plastic bag. Let stand in the refrigerator for half an hour before cooking.
- To make thick asparagus stalks tender, peel the lower parts up to the tender part with a potato peeler. Stalks taste as good as the flowers this way.

Beans

- To improve their texture and prevent mushiness and cracking, add a pinch of baking soda to the water when cooking dry beans. Never salt until beans are tender.

Beets

- To keep beets red, cook them whole with two inches of stem. Also add a few tablespoons of vinegar to the cooking water to prevent fading.

Broccoli

- A slice or two of stale bread in cooking water minimizes the cooking odor of broccoli. Skim the bread from the surface after cooking. This works with cabbage, too.
- Broccoli stems can be cooked in the same length of time as the flowerets if you make "X" incisions from top to bottom through stems.

Cabbage

- To reduce odor while cooking cabbage, place a small cup of vinegar on the range.
- Or add a wedge of lemon to the pot.
- To remove cabbage leaves more easily for stuffed-cabbage recipes, place the entire cabbage in water and bring it to a boil. Remove head, drain, and then pull off the leaves that have softened. Return the rest of the cabbage head to the water and repeat until all the leaves are soft enough to peel off.

Carrots
- Drop carrots in boiling water, let stand for five minutes, then drop them in cold water. The skin slips right off.
- Remember, remove the tops of carrots before storing in the refrigerator. Tops drain the carrots of moisture, making them limp and dry.

Cauliflower
- To keep cauliflower a bright white, add a little milk during cooking.
- Cauliflower odor is almost eliminated if you drop a few unshelled walnuts into the pot. Also works for cabbage odors.

Celery
- To make celery curls: Cut celery into three- to four-inch pieces. Cut each piece into narrow strips, leaving about an inch at the end uncut to hold the piece together, then put them in ice water until they curl, about half an hour.
- Cook a stalk or two of celery with broccoli, cabbage, and sauerkraut to prevent strong odors.
- And don't discard celery leaves: Dry them, then rub the leaves through a sieve for powder that can be used to flavor soups, stews, and salad dressings.

Corn on the cob
- Tastes much better when the tender green leaves from the corn are removed and used to line the bottom of the pot while corn is cooking.
- The easiest way to remove corn from the cob is to use an ordinary shoehorn.
- To remove corn silk: Dampen a toothbrush and brush downward on the cob of corn. Every strand should come off.
- And don't waste butter: Use a pastry brush to spread melted butter on corn. A celery stalk also makes an instant pastry brush.

Eggplant
- To rid eggplant of bitterness, drop it into salted water as you peel it. Pat it dry with a paper towel and it's ready to cook.
- A good rule of thumb: If eggplant is to be cooked for a short time, peel off the skin. If it is to be cooked longer, peeling isn't necessary.

Lettuce

- To perk up soggy lettuce, soak it for an hour in the refrigerator in a bowl of cold water and lemon juice. Douse quickly in hot and then ice water with a little apple-cider vinegar added.
- Lettuce or celery will crisp up quickly if you place it in a pan of cold water, adding a few slices of raw potato.

Lima beans

- For quick shelling, with scissors cut a thin strip along the inner edge of the pod, where the beans are attached.

Mushrooms

- Never immerse mushrooms in water when cleaning them because they will absorb too much water.
- To be sure you get prime mushrooms, buy only those with closed caps. The gills should not be showing.
- Keep mushrooms white and firm when sautéing them by adding a teaspoon of lemon juice to each quarter pound of melted butter.
- If mushrooms are too wet when cooking, they release too much moisture and steam instead of browning. Stirring the mushrooms with a long-handled fork and keeping fat very hot keep steam from building up.
- Use an egg slicer to slice fresh mushrooms quickly and uniformly.

Onions

- Keep onions whole when cooking them by cutting a small cross, one-quarter inch deep, in the stem end.
- Once an onion has been cut in half, rub the leftover cut side with butter and it will keep fresh longer.
- To make onions less strong, slice and separate them into rings, then soak them in cold water for one hour. (Mild onions are great for salads.)
- Peel fresh white onions easily by plunging them into boiling water for two minutes.
- Shed fewer tears:
  - Cut the root end of the onion off last.
  - Refrigerate onions before chopping.
  - Peel them under cold, running water.
  - Rinse hands frequently under cold water while chopping.
  - Keep your mouth tightly closed while chopping.
  - Chop with the exhaust fan operating.

Peas

- Always cook peas in the pod. The peas separate from the pods when cooked and the pods float to the surface. It's less work and the peas taste better.

Potatoes

Baked

- Rub butter or bacon fat over potatoes before baking to prevent skins from cracking and to improve the taste.
- To reheat leftover baked potatoes, dip them in hot water, then bake in 350° oven about twenty minutes.
- In a hurry? Boil potatoes in salted water for about ten minutes before popping them into a very hot oven.
- Or cut a thin slice from each end before popping them into the oven.
- To cut baking time by as much as half, place potatoes on the oven rack and place an iron pat over them.
- Or insert a nail to shorten baking time by fifteen minutes.

French fries
- For the best French fries, first let cut potatoes stand in cold water an hour before frying. Dry thoroughly before cooking. The trick is to fry them twice. The first time, just fry them for a few minutes and drain off grease. The second time, fry them until golden brown. There's no better way.

Mashed
- A well-beaten egg white added to mashed potatoes improves appearance and taste.
- Overcooked potatoes can become soggy when milk is added. Sprinkle with powdered milk or instant potatoes for the fluffiest mashed potatoes ever.

Potato pancakes
- To prevent discoloration, grate potatoes directly into a bowl of ice water.
- Or add a little sour cream to grated potatoes.
- And to use leftover mashed potatoes, coat patties with flour and fry them.

Potato-skin chips
- Potato skins cut into strips, seasoned, and baked in a hot oven make a nutritious snack.

Rehardening potatoes
- If your raw potatoes become soft, put them in ice water for half an hour and they'll become hard again.

Red cabbage
- To keep it from turning purple, add a tablespoon of vinegar when cooking red cabbage.

Rice
- For the whitest rice, add a few drops of lemon juice to the cooking water.

Sweet potatoes
- For simple peeling, take sweet potatoes from boiling water and plunge them immediately into cold water. The skins fall off.

Tomatoes

- Always add a pinch of sugar to tomatoes when cooking them. It enhances flavor.
- Slice tomatoes vertically and the slices stay firmer.
- Baked tomatoes and peppers hold their shape when baked in a greased muffin tin.
- To peel many tomatoes at once, place them in an old pillow case or onion netting bag and plunge them into a pot of boiling water for a minute. The skins slip right off.

Two in the time of one

- By wrapping each batch of two different vegetables separately in aluminum foil, you can cook both at the same time in just one pot. Save time, fuel, and cleanup.

Prevent vegetable boilovers

- A toothpick inserted between lid and pot before cooking will let just enough steam escape later to prevent messy boilovers.

Keep vegetables colorful

- Add a pinch of baking soda to cooking water.

Evicting the bugs

- To chase insects from cabbage, cauliflower, and similar vegetables, soak the vegetables in cold water with a few tablespoons of either salt or vinegar for fifteen minutes.

Frozen vegetables

- To restore a fresh flavor to frozen vegetables, pour boiling water over them to rinse away all traces of the frozen water.

Perking up vegetables

- If fresh vegetables are wilted or blemished, pick off the brown edges. Sprinkle vegetables with cool water, wrap them in a towel, and refrigerate for an hour or so.
- Many vegetables can be freshened by soaking them for an hour in cold water to which the juice of a lemon or a few tablespoons of vinegar have been added.

Eggs-pert-ease

Seeing through the shell
- Add food coloring to water before hard-boiling eggs, then you can tell the boiled eggs from the raw ones in the refrigerator.
- Or mark hard-boiled eggs with a crayon or pencil before storing.

Yolklore
- Keep yolks centered in eggs by stirring the water while cooking hard-boiled eggs. Especially good for deviled eggs.
- Keep yolk intact when separating it from the white by breaking the eggshell and tipping the whole egg into the palm of your hand. The yolk will remain in your palm while the egg white runs between your fingers and into a small bowl.
- You can cook whole yolks without their shells. Slide yolks gently into water and cook for about ten minutes. You can use yolks in salads or in a spread for hors d'oeuvre.
- Prevent crumbling yolks by dipping your knife or egg slicer in cold water before slicing hard-boiled eggs.
- Do not pour raw eggs or egg yolks directly into a hot mixture at once. Begin by adding a little of the hot mixture to the yolks first. Moderating the yolks' temperature this way prevents them from curdling when they are combined with the total hot mixture.

This is all it's "cracked" up to be
- You won't drop the eggs if you moisten your fingers before removing them from the carton.
- Boil cracked eggs in aluminum foil twisted at both ends.
- Rub a cut lemon over eggshells to keep them from breaking while cooking.
- Rescue an egg that cracks while boiling by immediately pouring a generous quantity of salt on the crack. This tends to seal the crack and contain the egg white.

- To peel hard-boiled eggs easily, plunge them into cold water. Crack the shell, then roll the egg lightly between the palms of your hands and the shell will come right off.
- Crack the shell of a boiled egg all over. Insert a small wet spoon between shell membrane and egg, then turn with the egg. Keep the spoon wet while you go. Perfect peeled egg every time!

Whites made right
- Beaten egg whites will be more stable if you add one teaspoon of cream of tartar to each batch of seven or eight egg whites.
- Let egg whites warm to room temperature before you beat them. Then, as you beat them, add slightly less than one tablespoon of water for each egg white to increase the volume.
- Egg whites will not beat satisfactorily if the least bit of yolk is present. Remove specks of yolk with a Q-tip or dampened cotton cloth, to which they will stick. Also make sure the egg beater is free of oil.
- A tablespoon of vinegar added to water before poaching eggs allows whites to set without spreading.

Just omelets
- For a stick-proof omelet pan, treat your pan right: Wipe the pan with paper toweling and table salt after each session of omelet-making.
- For a more tender omelet, add a small amount of water to the beaten eggs instead of milk or cream. Water retards coagulation of the yolks; milk or cream tends to harden them.

"Egg-stensions"
- If poached eggs can't be served immediately, put them in cool water and when you're ready to serve, reheat them gently in hot, salted water.
- For silky-smooth scrambled eggs, start with a cool, buttered pan and cook eggs very slowly. At the very end, stir in one tablespoon of cream or evaporated milk per portion.
- Or mix with a white sauce when serving a large crowd.

Please with Cheese

Hard facts
- To keep cheese from hardening, butter the cut end.
- To soften hardened cheese, soak it in buttermilk.
- Wrapping in aluminum foil also prevents dryouts.
- Store cheese in a wine-vinegar–soaked cloth for extra flavor and freshness.
- To prevent mold, store cheese in a tightly covered container with some sugar cubes.
- Cottage cheese will remain fresher longer if stored upside down in the refrigerator.

Grate hints
- Brush a little oil on the grater before you start grating, and cheese will wash off the grater easily.
- Force a soft cheese through a colander with a potato masher instead of grating it.
- Use a potato peeler to cut cheese into strips for salads and other garnishings.

Edge-wise
- A dull knife works much better than a sharp one for slicing cheese.
- Warm the knife before cutting cheese, and the cheese will cut as easily as butter.

Feats with Meats

Bringing home the bacon
- To keep bacon slices from sticking together, roll the package into a tube shape and secure it with a rubber band before refrigerating.
- Bacon fries with less curling if soaked a few minutes in cold water before frying.
- To help reduce shrinkage, put bacon slices in a cold skillet and prick them thoroughly with a fork as they fry.
- To make bacon curls, fry only until cooked but not crisp. Then take bacon from the skillet and twist around the tines of a fork. Pierce with a wooden toothpick and broil under a low flame to complete crisping.

Sausage links and patties
- Make sausage broiling easy by pressing several links onto a meat skewer—one flip turns them all.
- To prevent sausages from breaking or shrinking, boil them about eight minutes before they are fried. Or roll them lightly in flour before frying.
- Flouring sausage patties on both sides gives them an appetizing, crunchy crust as they fry. This method also helps prevent splattering.

Rounder burgers
- To get perfectly round meat patties, press down on flat patties with closed end of a No. 2½ can, then trim around the patty.

Juicier burgers
- Form patties around chunks of cracked ice; once on the grill, the melting ice will prevent overcooking. For a very moist burger, also put a few drops of cold water on both sides of the patty as you grill.
- Or add one stiffly beaten egg white for each pound of hamburger.
- Or add one grated large raw onion to each one and a half pounds of ground beef.
- Or make patties with one tablespoon of cottage cheese in the center.

Faster burgers

- Make lots of hamburgers for a large crowd by cooking in stacks. First, line baking pan with foil and arrange bottom tier of patties. Place another piece of foil over this layer and arrange the second tier. Stack them four deep. In a 350° oven, the patties will be thoroughly done in about thirty-five minutes. Do the same for frankfurters, but cook for only fifteen minutes.
- Or partially cook the meat, using the above method, and finish off on the outdoor grill.

For "loafers" only

- To keep hands clean, place all meat-loaf ingredients in a plastic bag, manipulate to mix and shape into a loaf, then slide loaf into pan.
- Meat loaf won't crack while baking if you rub cold water across the top of the meat before popping it into the oven.
- Instant potato flakes will bind and stretch your meat-loaf mixture.
- Make an "icing" of mashed potatoes to cover your meat loaf. Spread the mashed potatoes over the surface and lightly glaze with melted butter about fifteen minutes before the meat loaf is done. Then return meat to oven so the potato gets a light-brown crust.
- Baking meat loaf in a muffin tin rather than in a loaf pan reduces cooking time by as much as half.

Ham session

- Have your canned ham sliced by the butcher, then tie it back together, garnish with pineapple, and bake. No messy job of slicing it hot.
- Ham will be more tender and juicy if allowed to cool in the water in which it has been boiled.
- Ham will be deliciously moist if you empty a bottle of cola into the baking pan and bake the ham wrapped in aluminum foil. Remove the foil about half an hour before the ham is done, allowing the drippings to combine with the cola for a tasty brown gravy.
- For a too-salty ham, partially bake it and drain all the juices. Pour a small bottle of ginger ale over it and let it bake until done.

Roasts and steaks

- A shallow pan is better than a deep one for roasting because it allows heat to circulate around the roast.
- Instead of using a metal roasting rack, make a grid of carrot and celery sticks and place meat or poultry on it. The additional advantage: Vegetables flavor the pan drippings.
- To prevent meat from scorching when roasting, place a pan of cold water in the oven.
- For easier slicing, let a roast stand for ten to fifteen minutes after removing it from the oven.
- And when broiling a steak, add a cup of water to the bottom portion of the pan before sliding it into the oven. The water helps absorb smoke and grease.

Lick your chops

- For tasty, greaseless pork chops, line a loaf pan with sliced bread and add browned chops, standing them up in the pan so that they lean against the bread. Cover with foil and bake. Grease is absorbed by bread.

Lamb glamour

- With toothpicks, fasten a piece of garlic bread, butter side down, to the meat. Sprinkle with water and roast. Garlic butter gives the meat a snappy flavor, and the bread makes an appetizing dressing.
- Or baste the roasting lamb with a cup of hot coffee containing cream and sugar.

For high livers
- Liver will be especially tender if first soaked in milk. Refrigerate meat about two hours, remove, dry thoroughly, bread and sauté.
- Or try soaking it in tomato juice for two to three hours before broiling or frying.

Tough meats
- Tenderize tough meat by rubbing all sides with a mixture of vinegar and olive oil. Let it stand two hours before cooking.
- For a very tough piece of meat, rub it well with baking soda, let stand a few hours, then wash it thoroughly before cooking.
- When pounding to tenderize meat, pound flour into it to prevent the juices from escaping.

Stop the splattering
- To keep hot fat from splattering, first sprinkle a little salt in the frying pan.

Gravy training
- Mix cold water and flour or cornstarch into a smooth paste. Cover the jar and shake it until the paste is smooth. Add mixture gradually to the pan, stirring the gravy constantly while bringing it to a boil.
- A quick way to darken gravy: Mix one tablespoon of sugar and one tablespoon of water and heat the mixture in a heavy pan until the water evaporates and the sugar starts to brown. Then pour the pale gravy into the sugared pan.
- Or add dark, percolated coffee to pale gravy. It will add color but won't affect the taste.
- For greaseless gravy: Pour pan drippings into a tall glass; the grease will rise to the top in minutes. Remove it and prepare grease-free gravy.
- Add one-quarter teaspoon of baking soda to greasy gravy.
- Buzz lumpy gravy in your blender.

Birds of a Feather

Freshness
- Never buy chicken on Monday. It is likely you'll get one that wasn't bought by the weekend.
- To keep fresh chicken fresher, immediately remove polyethylene wrap, loosely wrap chicken in waxed paper, and refrigerate. Fresh chicken should be used within three days.

No more fowl play
- Defrost a frozen chicken by soaking it in cold water that's been heavily salted. This draws out blood, and the breast meat will be pure white.
- An unpleasant poultry odor can be neutralized if you wash the bird with the juice of half a lemon, then rub it with salt and lemon.

A time saver
- Debone chicken with a pair of kitchen scissors. It is easier than hacking and whacking with a knife.

Chicken scoops

- After flouring chicken, chill for one hour. The coating will adhere better during frying.
- Marinate chicken breasts in milk, cream, or buttermilk for three hours in the refrigerator before frying or baking to ensure tenderness.
- For an especially light and delicate crust on coated fried foods, add about three-quarters of a teaspoon of baking powder to the batter and use club soda for the liquid.
- Chicken bastes itself when you roast it covered with bacon slices. Do not butter.

Deep frying

- To test whether hot oil is still usable, drop a piece of white bread into the pan. If the bread develops dark specks, the oil is deteriorating.
- When reusing frying oil, eliminate odors and unwanted taste by first frying a dozen sprigs of parsley or a raw potato in the oil for about fifteen minutes.

Dumplings

- Slice a stack of flour tortillas into one-inch strips and add to a simmering stew ten minutes before the stew is done. This is cheap, easy, and good enough to fool dumpling experts.
- To resist the "sneak peak" temptation when making real dumplings, cover pot with a glass pie plate while dumplings are cooking.

Talking turkey

- Buy a large turkey when it's on sale and have butcher cut it in half. Each part still has white and dark meat and a cavity for stuffing.
- Instead of one large turkey, buy two small ones. They will roast in much less time and you'll have a larger portion of the better cuts of meats.
- Unwaxed dental floss is good for trussing because it does not burn and is very strong.
- Or, instead of sewing a stuffed turkey, close the cavity with two heels of dampened bread. Push each into an opening with crust facing out and overlapping to hold the stuffing in.
- Or close the cavity with one or two raw potatoes.

- Instead of stuffing a bird, try steaming it by pouring one cup of water mixed with one-quarter cup of pineapple juice into the body cavity. The meat will be more flavorful and juicy.
- Always roast turkey in roasting pan with breast side down to prevent the white meat from getting dry. Turn breast up during the last hour of cooking.

"I've got juice under my skin"
- For a juicier bird, fill a basting needle with one-quarter pound of melted margarine. Inject into raw turkey around breast and thigh in six to eight places.

When
the Dish Is Fish

From fin to finish
- You can tell a fresh fish by checking to see if the eyes are bright, clear, and slightly protruding. A stale fish has sunken, cloudy, or pink eyes. Make sure the scales are shiny and tight against the skin. Examine the gills: They should be red or pink, never gray.
- If in doubt about the freshness of a fish, place it in cold water. If it floats, it's probably just been caught.
- Make your own fish scaler by nailing several bottle caps to the end of a piece of wood, three bottle caps wide and eight inches long. The serrated edges will provide a fine scaling surface.
- Before scaling, rub the entire fish with vinegar and the scales will come off in a snap.
- Sprinkle some salt on a board when cleaning fish to keep it from slipping.
- After cleaning a fish, bend and roll it at each section and the bones will pierce through. Be careful not to tear fish when pulling the bones out.
- And to remove the bones easily after cooking, first rub melted butter down the back of the fish to be cooked.

More fish tips

- A dash of lemon juice and milk added to the seasoned liquid in which halibut or another white fish is cooked makes flesh white.
- Baking fish on a bed of chopped onion, celery, and parsley not only makes the fish taste better but also keeps it from sticking to the pan.
- Thaw frozen fish in milk. The milk draws out the frozen taste and provides a fresh-caught flavor.
- Try soaking fish in one-quarter cup of vinegar, wine, or lemon juice and water before cooking to make it sweet and tender.
- Use a piece of foil that's been crumpled and then smoothed out to bake fish sticks. Turn them over as required. They will brown equally on bottom and top and won't stick, either.
- Soak saltwater fish in vinegar to eliminate some of the salty taste. Then rinse fish under cold water.

Odor eaters

- To remove fish odor from hands, rub them with vinegar or salt.
- To reduce fish smell, put a dash of vinegar in the poaching liquid. Adding sesame oil before cooking also works.
- To rid frying pans of fish odor, sprinkle salt in the pan, add hot water, and let stand awhile before rinsing.

Shrimp primping

- After shelling and deveining shrimp, put them in a bowl and wash gently under cold, running water for half a minute. Next, rinse them in a colander under briskly running cold water for about three minutes. When cooked, they will almost crunch.
- Never boil shrimp, it makes them rubbery. Instead, after running them under cold water, put shrimp in pot with a dash of salt and cover with boiling water. Stir a few minutes, then put lid on tightly over pot. Very large shrimp are ready to eat in six minutes, average size in four, and small in three. The secret of perfection is that the pot is never set over the heat.
- Canned shrimp lose their "canned taste" if you soak them for fifteen minutes in two tablespoons of vinegar and a teaspoon of sherry.

Open-and-shut oyster case

- If you soak oysters in club soda for about five minutes, they are usually more easily removed from their shells.
- Clams and oysters are simple to open if first washed with cold water, then put into a plastic bag and kept in the freezer for half an hour.
- Or drop them into boiling water and let them stand for a few minutes. This relaxes their muscles and makes them easy to open with a knife or beer-can opener.

Using Your Noodle

Preventing boilovers

- Lay a large spoon or spatula across the top of the pot to reduce boilovers and splashing while cooking.
- Or first rub shortening around the top of the pot.
- Or add a pat of butter or a few teaspoons of cooking oil to the water. This method also prevents pasta from sticking together.

Perfect pasta

- Bring salted water to a boil, stir in pasta, cover pot, and turn off heat. Let sit for fifteen minutes or until done.
- When done, run cooked spaghetti under hot—not cold—water before draining to prevent stickiness.
- If pasta is to be used in a dish that requires further cooking, such as lasagna, reduce pasta cooking time by one-third.
- If you're not going to serve spaghetti immediately, you can leave it in hot water if you add enough ice cubes or cold water to stop the cooking process. Reheat spaghetti by running it under hot tap water in the strainer while shaking it vigorously.

Three steps in one
- Use your French-fry basket or a large strainer when cooking pasta. It is so easy to lift the basket out of the water before rinsing the pasta and transferring it to the serving bowl.

The best way to store
- After opening a box of any pasta product, store unused portion in a tightly covered glass container to preserve freshness.

Are you a noodle maker?
- If you make your own noodles, drape the noodles over an old-fashioned wooden collapsible clothes hanger to dry.

Pizza with pizzazz
- Try hard-wheat flour or pasta flour (available at health-food stores) for the best golden-brown pizza crust.
- Slice or grate the cheese and put it directly on the dough, under the sauce. Your pizza crust will get crispy without the cheese burning. Also keeps the crust from getting soggy.
- Pizza cuts more easily with scissors.

In Your Cups:
Beverages

Ground rules for cutting coffee costs
- Grind beans until coffee is very fine, or use a food processor. You'll need about one-third less coffee than you ordinarily would.
- Use half as much ground coffee as you usually use, and pour water through grounds an extra time.
- Reuse old coffee grounds by placing them in the oven on a flat pan for half an hour at 350°. Then combine with half the usual amount of fresh-ground coffee.
- Coffee too weak? Add a little instant coffee to the pot.

Café mocha for half the cost

- Add one-half envelope of instant cocoa mix to one cup of strong black coffee.
- Put a piece of chocolate or a vanilla bean in the coffee filter before you add the coffee for a special flavor.

Filter tips

- Paper towels cut to size make inexpensive filters for percolators or drip pots.
- Remove some of the acid taste of coffee by adding a small pinch of salt before pouring in the boiling water. Works for hot chocolate, too!
- For clear coffee, put unwashed egg shells in after percolating coffee. Remember, always start with cold water.

Cream scheme

- When out of cream, try the beaten white of an egg in your coffee.
- A tiny pinch of baking soda in cream keeps it from curdling in hot coffee.

Just your cup of tea

- Add delicious fragrance and flavor to tea by keeping a few pieces of dried orange rind or dried orange blossoms in the tea canister.
- Prevent tea from getting cloudy by adding a pinch of baking soda per pot.
- Flavor tea by using sugar cubes that have been dipped in orange or lemon juice.
- If you like sweet tea, add powdered lemonade mix or dissolve old-fashioned lemon drops in your tea.

Hot chocolate

- Skin won't form on the top of hot chocolate if you beat the drink until frothy immediately after preparation.
- Add, per pot, a pinch of salt and a teaspoon of cornstarch dissolved in a little water to improve the flavor and texture of hot chocolate. Try adding a marshmallow dipped in cinnamon to each cup.

Fizzlers

- To reduce foam when pouring carbonated drinks over ice cubes, rinse off ice cubes with water before filling glasses.
- Use club soda instead of water for a bubbly Kool-Aid drink.
- Prepare frozen juice concentrate as directed. Fill glass half full and mix with club soda for a nutritious soda pop.

Juice spruce-ups

- Improve the taste of an ordinary large can of tomato juice by pouring it into a glass bottle and adding one green onion and one stalk of celery cut into small pieces. After it stands for a while, it tastes like the more expensive, already seasoned juice.
- Keep juice cold without watering it down by putting a tightly closed plastic bag of ice into the pitcher.
- Frozen orange juice will have a fresh-squeezed flavor if you add the juice of two fresh oranges to the reconstituted frozen juice.
- To thaw frozen juice in a hurry, spin concentrate with water in a blender for a few seconds.

An Ounce
of Prevention

Safety "firsts"

- Keep cold water running in the sink while you pour hot water from a pot of vegetables. It prevents the steam from scalding your hands.
- Don't let oil heat to the smoking point. It may ignite. (It also makes food taste bitter and irritates your eyes.)
- Sharp knives should be kept in plain view in wooden holders—but out of the reach of young children—instead of among other utensils in drawer.
- When broiling meat, place a few pieces of dry bread in the broiler pan to soak up dripping fat. This not only eliminates smoking fat but also reduces the chance that the fat will catch fire.

Quick help for burns
- To help relieve pain from minor burns and reduce swelling of minor bumps and bruises, keep clean, damp sponges in your freezer. When you burn or bruise yourself, apply a frozen sponge to the affected area.
- Soothe a minor kitchen burn by rubbing it gently with the cut surface of a cold raw potato.
- Or dissolve baking powder in cold water to make a paste. Apply to burn and cover with clean gauze.
- To relieve painful burns on hands, dissolve a few aspirin tablets in a bowl of cool water and soak.

In case of fire
- Sprinkle bicarbonate of soda over grease flare-up or blazing broiler. If fire is snuffed out quickly, a partially burned steak may still be edible after the soda is rinsed off.
- NOTE: Never use flour as an extinguisher.
- If fire is in oven, immediately turn off heat and close the oven door. Shutting off the air supply will smother the fire.

The Best of Helpful Kitchen Hints for
Baking

Breadtime Story

When you knead a lot of dough
- Oil hands a little, and hard-to-knead dough, such as pumpernickel, whole wheat, and rye, will be easier to handle.
- To keep the bowl from slipping and sliding while mixing ingredients, place it on a folded damp towel.
- The tenderness and flakiness of biscuit dough and pie pastry depend on finely cut cold lard mixed with flour. To keep the fat from melting, handle biscuit dough as little as possible.
- Dough won't stick to hands if it is kneaded inside a large plastic bag. Neither will it stick to the bag or dry out.

Or care about the upper crust
- Press dough into a greased bowl, turn to bring it greased side up, and cover; then the dough won't form a crust while rising in the bowl.
- To brown the sides of a loaf almost as well as the top, use a dull-finish aluminum, dark metal, or glass pan for baking.
- To get the dull finish on a shiny new pan, first use it for something other than baking bread, or bake it empty in a 350° oven.
- Your bread will be crusty if the top and sides are brushed with an egg white diluted with one tablespoon of water.
- A small pan of water in the oven keeps crusts from getting too hard when baking. Spread warm crust with soft butter for a soft crust on freshly baked bread.

Or like it hot
- Place aluminum foil under the napkin in your roll basket and the rolls will stay hot longer.

Or cool
- Let baked bread cool on rack rather than in the pan. Cooling in the pan makes sides and bottom soggy.

Rise to the occasion
- Use water in which potatoes have been boiled to make yeast breads moister. The texture may be coarser, but the bread lasts longer and is slightly larger.

- Add half a teaspoon of sugar to the yeast when stirring it into the water to dissolve. If in ten minutes the mixture bubbles and foams, the yeast is alive and kicking. Or test by putting one teaspoon into a cup of hot water. If it fizzles actively, use it.
- In a cool room: Set the pan of dough in an unheated oven over smaller pan of hot water.
- Or, before baking, put the dough in a container on a heating pad set on medium. The heating pad makes dough rise perfectly.

- If the TV is in use, let the dough rise on top of the set. It's a good source of warmth—and if you're watching a program, you won't forget about the dough.
- Speed up slow-rising dough by putting the bowl with the dough in a large plastic bag; fold the ends of plastic under the bowl.

Put on a shiny face

- Brush a mixture of one tablespoon of sugar and one-quarter cup of milk on rolls before popping them into the oven for a really tip-top glaze.
- For a shiny crust, before putting the bread in the oven, brush the top of the loaf with a mixture of one egg beaten with one tablespoon of milk.

Smooth away wrinkles

- For wrinkled buns, moisten them slightly and heat in 350° oven for a few minutes. No more wrinkles.

Let Them Eat Cake

Better batters
- A beaten egg added slowly to batter prevents the batter from becoming too stiff.
- If you must use all-purpose flour for cake, use seven-eighths of a cup for every cup of cake flour called for. Sift twice to make it lighter.
- To cut down on cholesterol, for each whole egg called for in a recipe, substitute two egg whites stiffly beaten and folded into the cake batter.
- A little flour mixed into the remains of melted chocolate in the pan will get the last bit of chocolate out of the pan and into the cake batter.
- Two tablespoons of salad oil added to cake mix keeps the mix moist and less crumbly.
- Heat nuts, fruits, and raisins in the oven before adding them to cake and pudding batter. That way, they won't be as likely to sink to the bottom of the cake. Fruits and raisins may also be rolled in butter before being added; or put them in hot water for a few minutes. Sprinkle frozen berries, such as raspberries, in cinnamon sugar before adding them to cake batter for a great taste and an even distribution of berries throughout the cake.

Watch my dust
- Use cocoa to dust baking tins so cookies and cakes won't have that floury look.
- Or dust your prepared cake pans with some of the dry cake mix when making a box cake.

Pan plans
- Trace the outline of the baking-pan bottom on waxed paper and cut it out. Grease and flour the sides of the pan only and place the waxed-paper cutout on the bottom of the pan. Pour in the batter. After baking, when you remove the cake from the pan, it won't stick. Gently peel off waxed paper while the cake is still warm.
- Grease pans with a smooth mixture of oil, shortening, and flour to keep cakes from sticking to the tins.

- New tins should be greased and put in a moderate oven for fifteen minutes to prevent burned cake bottoms.
- Take cake out of the oven and set it briefly on a damp cloth to make the cake come loose from the pan.
- If the cake sticks to the pan and seems about to split, hold the pan over a low flame for five to eight seconds and the cake will come out nice and firm.

Done right by me

- If the top of your cake is browning too quickly, place a pan of warm water on the rack above the cake while it is baking in the oven.
- If toothpicks are too short to test a cake for "doneness," a piece of uncooked spaghetti does the job.
- A freshly baked cake that's too high in the center may be flattened to the right shape by pressing the bottom of a slightly smaller pan down onto it. It won't hurt the cake.
- A cake rack covered by a paper towel lets the cake "breathe" as it cools. The cake won't stick to the paper towel, either.
- To keep cake from cracking when baked, avoid overbeating. Too much air in the batter causes cracking.

Serving you right

- If a cake is to be cut while hot, use unwaxed dental floss instead of a knife.
- To cut cake without breaking the icing, wet your knife in boiling water before beginning the job.
- To eliminate mess, freeze your unfrosted cake before cutting it into decorative party shapes. Your cake will slice evenly, too.
- Before adding bananas to cake or pie, dip them in fruit juice and they won't burn.
- Freeze, then thaw an angel-food cake for neat slices and no crumbs.

Flavor savors

- For a moist and fluffy chocolate cake, try adding a spoonful of vinegar to the baking soda.
- When a recipe calls for chocolate slivers, you can make the finest shavings of chocolate yourself. A chocolate bar and a potato peeler will do the trick cheaply and conveniently.
- By adding a pinch of salt to dishes containing chocolate you enhance the flavor.
- To melt chocolate without scorching, always melt it in the top of a double boiler. If it starts to harden after melting, add enough vegetable oil to liquefy.
- Use orange juice instead of water to make a sponge cake more flavorful.

Re-fresher course

- Wrap cake tightly in transparent plastic wrap and let it stand about a day before serving for that extra tenderness.
- To preserve the creamy texture, thaw frozen cheesecake in the refrigerator for twelve hours.
- When storing cake, place half an apple in the container along with the cake to retain freshness.
- Or fasten a slice of fresh bread with toothpicks to the cut edge of a cake to keep the cake from drying out and getting stale.
- Dip stale cake quickly in cold milk and heat in a moderate oven.

Tips to top it off

- To prevent hardening and cracking, add a pinch of baking powder when making a powdered-sugar icing. It will stay moist.
- To prevent icings from becoming granular, add a pinch of salt to the sugar.
- Icing a many-layered cake is easier when you secure the layers by inserting a few sticks of dry spaghetti through them as you go. No more sliding before the icing sets.
- To make your own cake decorator, roll a piece of paper into a cone shape so that one end has a smaller opening than the other. Snip the small end with scissors to make a good point. Put icing in and squeeze it out through the pointed end. A plastic bag will also work well.
- Powdered sugar sprinkled on top of each cake layer before frosting or filling prevents filling from soaking through the cake.
- Try using devil's-food cake mix instead of cocoa in frostings.
- For a delicious frosting, top each cupcake with a marshmallow two minutes before removing pan from the oven.
- If frosting becomes too hard or stiff as you are beating it, beat in some lemon juice.
- To light birthday candles, use a lit piece of uncooked spaghetti as a punk.

Smooth, soft, and so good

- To make a smooth-looking frosting, first frost cake with a thin layer of icing. When this "base coat" sets, apply a second, final coat. It goes on easily and looks superb.
- To keep fudge frosting soft and workable, keep frosting in a bowl in a pan of hot water. Add one teaspoon of cornstarch for the smoothest frosting yet.
- An instant and delicious frosting for cakes and other desserts is made by adding a little chocolate syrup to a prepared whipped topping.

Hello, doily

- For a fast topping for cakes, place a paper doily with a large design on top of the cake, then dust powdered sugar over it lightly. Lift doily off gently.

Doughnut do's

- The more egg yolk you use in doughnuts, the less grease the doughnuts will absorb.
- Or let the doughnuts stand for fifteen minutes or so before frying them; they'll absorb less fat.
- Dip doughnuts quickly in boiling water after removing them from oil. Drain as usual. They'll be less greasy.
- A few slices of potato added to the grease will keep doughnuts from burning.
- Stale doughnuts become breakfast treats when you split them, then dip them in French-toast batter and brown them in butter.
- Use a potato parer or a grater to remove burned crusts.
- For quick and easy doughnuts, use the cap from the cooking-oil bottle to make holes in the center of each biscuit roll from a tube of prepared refrigerator dough. Fry as you would homemade doughnuts, drain, cool, and roll in sugar or frost.

Flaky ideas

- For the flakiest upper pie crust, just brush the top crust lightly with cold water before baking. The crust will melt in your mouth.
- Use ice water in making pie and pastry crust. The cold keeps the shortening intact and makes the pastry flakier.
- Another good way to keep pie crust from becoming soggy is to sprinkle it with equal parts of sugar and flour before adding filling.
- A "nuttier" method is to spread finely ground nuts over the bottom crust. This keeps the crust from becoming soggy and adds a delicious flavor.
- Lard is better than vegetable shortening for making pie dough. While butter imparts a better flavor, it also melts easily when the dough is handled and makes the crust less flaky.
- Brush the unbaked bottom crust of your pie with well-beaten egg white before filling. This keeps berries and other fruits from making pie bottoms mushy.
- Before filling, place pies in a very hot oven for the first ten minutes to firm the lower crust.
- Brush your pie lightly with milk before baking to give it a rich brown glaze.
- Brush your frozen pies with melted butter before baking. The butter eliminates the dryness that freezing causes.
- Rolling pins or pastry boards should be scraped with a knife or scraper—never washed. This prevents dough from sticking the next time around.

Facts about fillings

- When fresh fruit is plentiful and you don't have the time to make the whole pie, try this: Mix the fruit as you would in preparing a pie. Put the pie filling in several pie pans lined with waxed paper or aluminum foil. Cover and freeze. When you have time to prepare crusts or if you want to fill a frozen pie crust, just pop your pie-shaped fillings into the crust and bake.
- Add a spoonful of tapioca to pie fillings that contain especially juicy fruits. The tapioca absorbs the excess juice and keeps the filling in the crust.

- Moisten a narrow strip of cloth with cold water and fit it around the edge of a juicy pie to keep the juice from overflowing.
- Add a beaten egg white to sugar used for juicy fruit pies to prevent juice from spreading when pie is served, or lightly beat a whole egg and add a little flour to the fruit for pies.

Vent-sures
- Before baking, insert tube-type macaroni in the center of the top of your pie so that juice can bubble out.
- Or cut a paper drinking straw into three pieces and place them in the center of the pie for the same effect.

Mile-high meringues
- For the highest meringue, the secret is to add some baking powder to room-temperature egg whites before beating them.
- For a meringue that won't stick when it's cut, sift a little sugar over the top of the pie just before it browns.
- Or butter the knife first.
- Or dip the knife in boiling water before cutting the pie and the meringue won't crumble.
- For a higher, more stable meringue, add one teaspoon of lemon juice for every three egg whites.
- Always spread meringue all the way to the edge of the pie crust. This prevents shrinking and watery edges.
- If you turn off your oven and open the door slightly when the meringue is just perfectly brown, the pie cools slowly and prevents the meringue from cracking or splitting.

Here's the Way
the Cookie Crumbles

Coping with cookie sheets
- If you have no cookie sheet or you need extras, turn a baking pan upside down and drop the dough on the bottom.
- To keep cookies from burning on the bottom, cool the cookie sheet before reusing. Run cold water over the back of sheet only, then dry and bake the next batch.
- When cookies stick to the cookie sheet, run the sheet over a gas burner. If this doesn't work, return cookies to the oven for a few minutes.
- Or remove soft and sticky cookies from the cookie sheet with a greased spatula.
- Or rub a piece of crumpled waxed paper over warm cookie sheet and repeat after each batch.

Breaking up is hard to do
- To break up lumpy brown sugar and make it easier to cream into butter or margarine for cookie dough, run it in blender until it becomes soft and fluffy.
- Or grate it.

Dealing with cookie dough

- To make rolled cookies thinner and crisper, roll the dough directly on the bottom of a greased and floured cookie sheet. Cut the dough into shapes and remove the extra dough from between them.
- Or put cookies by teaspoonsful on baking sheet. Press with the bottom of a water glass that's first been dipped in sugar each time.

Cookie coating

- To add a crispy coating to cookies, sprinkle a mixture of flour and sugar on the pastry board before rolling out the dough.
- Or add a nuttier flavor by toasting oatmeal topping first. Sprinkle it over a pan and place in the oven, at low temperature, for ten to fifteen minutes.
- Brush the surface with slightly beaten egg yolk thinned with water. Once the coating dries, you can leave as is or paint on some designs.
- To keep molasses cookies soft, add a little cream cheese to the frosting. Not too much, or the frosting tastes cheesy.
- Take cookies out two minutes before baking time is up and they'll continue baking right on the hot sheet pan—and will never overbake.
- Crumble stale, hard cookies, save them in a jar, and use for toppings for coffee cakes or for a pie crust instead of graham crackers.
- To keep cookies moist, keep bread or an apple in the cookie jar.

Cookie cutting

- By dipping the cookie cutter in slightly warm salad oil you get a much cleaner cut. This works especially well with plastic cutters.
- Pack homemade refrigerator cookie dough into large juice cans and freeze. Thaw fifteen minutes, open the bottom, and push up. Use the edge as a cutting guide.

Sweet send-offs

- The best way to cushion cookies for mailing is with popcorn.
- Stale angel-food cake can be turned into delicious cookies. Shape half-inch slices with a cookie cutter, toast the "cookies," and frost with glaze or icing.

Just Desserts

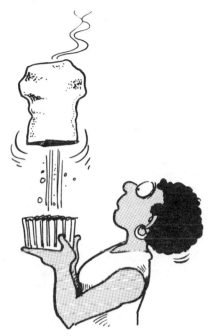

Keep it light

- For a lighter soufflé, fashion a collar from brown or waxed paper or aluminum foil, butter it well, and wrap it about five inches high around soufflé mold. Tie with twine, then pour soufflé mixture into dish. Uncollar before serving.
- To bake a soufflé with a soft center, cook it in a slightly hotter oven and for a shorter time than the recipe recommends. When the top is brown, remove the soufflé from the oven.
- For a lighter steamed pudding, substitute bread crumbs for half the flour.
- Skin won't form on puddings if you place plastic wrap directly on its surface.
- To keep baked custards and puddings from becoming watery, place the baking dish in a pan of water in the oven during baking. The water should be halfway up the dish.
- Spread a thin layer of melted butter or cream over jellies, puddings, and sauces right after cooking. Stir—all the skin and foam will disappear.

- For lighter crêpes, use three parts skim milk and one part water. Using just milk or light cream for the liquid makes a heavier crêpe.
- For perfectly thin and tender crêpes, use just enough batter to cover the bottom of the pan. A thin, thin layer is the secret.

Pancake makeup
- For the lightest pancakes ever, replace liquid in pancakes and waffles with club soda. Use up all the batter; do not store. Close windows before cooking or pancakes may float out!
- Store extra pancakes or waffles in plastic bags in your freezer. Just pop them in the toaster to heat.
- Add several tablespoons of your favorite jam or preserves to one cup of light corn syrup. Heat and serve as pancake topping.

For wonderful whipping cream
- Chill cream, bowl, and beater well.
- Whip cream in a double boiler over ice cubes and salt. It will whip faster and have more body.
- For stubborn cream, gradually whip in three or four drops of lemon juice.
- Add the white of an egg. Chill, then whip.
- Preserve the firm shape of whipped cream by using powdered sugar instead of granulated sugar. The whipped cream won't get watery.
- Cream whipped ahead of time will not separate if you add a touch of unflavored gelatin (one-quarter teaspoon per cup of cream).
- Cover the top of the bowl with a piece of waxed paper in which a hole has been cut for the beater.

Tiptop toppings
- Just as you remove hot baked apples from the oven, top with honey. The honey will be absorbed fully by the apple and won't burn during baking.
- To make a strawberry glaze, mix two tablespoons of strawberry juice, one-quarter cup of sugar, one tablespoon of lemon juice, and stir until sugar is dissolved.

The Best of Helpful Kitchen Hints for
Fruits

The Fruits of Success

Peels off pronto

- Place *thin-skinned* fruits in a bowl, cover with boiling water, and let sit for one minute. Peel with a paring knife.
- Or spear the fruit on a long-handled fork and hold over.a gas flame until the skin cracks. Then peel it.
- To peel *thick-skinned fruits,* cut a sliver of peel from the top and bottom. Then set fruit on a cutting board, cut end down. Using a knife, cut off the peel in strips from top to bottom.

Preparing cut fruit ahead of time

- Keep fruit from turning brown by dissolving two crushed vitamin-C tablets in a bowl of cool water before adding fruit.
- Toss freshly cut fruit in lemon juice and it won't darken. The juice of half a lemon is enough for a quart or two of cut fruits.
- For fruits cut in two, brush surfaces with lemon juice to prevent discoloration.

Apples

- Apples keep longer if you make sure they don't touch one another.
- When baking apples, remove a horizontal slice of peel from around the middle. Apples won't shrink while baking.
- Wrinkled skins can be avoided by cutting slits in a few places before baking.
- Soak cut apple pieces in salted water for ten minutes. They'll remain crispy and won't turn brown.
- Dried-out apples will regain their flavor if you cut them up and sprinkle the pieces with apple cider.
- For winter storage, wipe apples dry and pack in dry sand or sawdust. Keep in cool, dry place.

Avocados

- Avocados ripen quickly when put in a brown paper bag and set in a warm place.
- Test for ripeness by sticking a toothpick in the fruit at the stem end. If it goes in and out easily, the fruit is ripe and ready to eat.
- If ripe, store avocados in the refrigerator.

Bananas

- Ripen green bananas more quickly by placing them near an overripe banana.
- Or wrap green bananas in a wet dish towel and put them in a paper sack.
- Store bananas in the refrigerator after they have ripened. The cold, although it turns the skin dark brown, does no damage to the fruit inside and helps slow down further ripening.
- And bananas will keep much longer if stored in the refrigerator in a tightly closed jar. Do *not* peel the skin.

Berries

- Before purchasing, check the bottom of the berry container to make sure it is not badly stained from mushy or moldy fruit. If stained badly, forget it; the berries aren't fresh.
- When you get home, separate the bruised and spoiled berries from the good ones because mold spreads quickly from berry to berry.
- Do not wash or hull any berries until you're ready to eat them.

Cranberries

- Add one teaspoon of butter to each pound of cranberries when cooking them to eliminate foam and overboiling.
- If you add one-quarter teaspoon of soda to cranberries while cooking them, they'll need less sugar.
- Cook cranberries just until they pop. Further cooking makes them taste bitter.

Strawberries

- Strawberries can be kept firm for several days if you store them in a colander in the refrigerator, which allows the cold air to circulate around them.
- Never hull strawberries until they have been washed or they will absorb too much water and become mushy.

Cantaloupe

- *Study it!* The skin color should be yellow-green to creamy yellow—not green.
- *Shake it!* If it's really ripe, you can hear the seeds rattling inside.
- *Smell it!* It should give off a fragrance.
- *Feel it!* The "belly button" should be somewhat soft. If the melon is soft all over, it is probably overripe.

Grapefruit

- The thickness—not the color—of the skin tells you a lot about the quality of the fruit. Thin-skinned fruits are probably juicier than thick-skinned ones. Thick-skinned fruits are usually pointed at the stem end and look rough and wrinkled.
- Let grapefruit stand in boiling water for a few minutes and see how much more easily they'll peel.

Lemons

- Look for lemons with the smoothest skin and the smallest points on each end. They have more juice and a better flavor.
- Submerging a lemon in hot water for fifteen minutes before squeezing it will yield almost twice the amount of juice.

- Or warm lemons in your oven for a few minutes before squeezing them.
- Or roll a lemon on a hard surface, pressing with your hand.
- If you need only a few drops of juice, prick one end with a fork and squeeze the desired amount. Return the lemon to refrigerator and it will be good as new.

Oranges
- The color of an orange is no indication of its quality because oranges are usually dyed to improve their appearance.
- Brown spots on the skin indicate a good-quality orange.
- Pick a sweet orange by examining the navel. Choose the ones with the biggest holes.
- If you put oranges in a hot oven before peeling them, no white fibers will be left on them.
- To increase juice yield, follow hints for lemons (above).

Peaches
- Peaches ripen quickly if you put them in a box covered with newspaper. Gases are sealed in.
- Skins come off smoothly if peach is peeled with a potato peeler.
- Remember when peaches had a fuzzy topcoat? What happened to all that peach fuzz? Today, peaches are defuzzed by a mechanical brushing process before shipment.

Pears
- Ripen pears quickly by placing them in a brown paper bag along with a ripe apple. Set in a cool, shady spot and make sure a few holes are punched into the bag. The ripe apple gives off a gas, ethylene, which stimulates the other fruit to ripen. The ripe-apple trick has the same effect on peaches and tomatoes.

Pineapple

- Don't use fresh pineapple in gelatin desserts. It contains an enzyme that prevents gelatin from setting. In gelatin, use either the canned product or fresh pineapple that has been parboiled for five minutes.
- When pineapple isn't quite ripe, remove top and skin, slice, and place in pot. Cover with water and add sugar to taste. Boil a few minutes, cool, and refrigerate. Fruit tastes fresh and crunchy.

Raisins

- Chopping raisins is easier to do if you put a thin film of butter on both sides of the chopping knife.
- Raisins won't stick to food chopper if they are soaked in cold water for a short time before grinding.

Watermelon

- To test for ripeness, snap thumb and third finger against the melon. If it says *pink* in a high, shrill tone, the melon isn't ripe. If you hear *punk* in a deep, low voice, the melon is ready to eat.

The Best of Helpful Kitchen Hints for
Spices

Come Let Us Season Together

Bay leaves
- Place bay leaves in a tea ball for easy removal from a stew before serving.
- Or skewer with a toothpick, making it easy to spot them. The same applies for any other herbs, such as garlic cloves, that don't dissolve as they cook.

Capsicum
- Spices from the Capsicum genus include paprika, red pepper (cayenne), and chili powder. During hot summer months store these in dark containers on the refrigerator-door compartments; they deteriorate in heat and high humidity.
- The best way to store hot chilies is in the refrigerator in a porous brown paper bag, loosely sealed. They will retain their potency for days.

Chives
- To chop chives, a chopping board isn't necessary. Take chives from the freezer and grate only enough for use, returning the remainder to the freezer. That way chives taste the same as when freshly chopped. Do the same with parsley.

Cinnamon
- Add one teaspoon of cinnamon as a "secret ingredient" for deep-fried beer-batter chicken.

Cloves
- Hang an orange stuck with whole cloves in your closet to keep the air fresh and fragrant.

Fresh herbs
- Keep fresh herbs flavorful by soaking them in olive oil; then refrigerate.
- Triple the amount of fresh herbs used in place of dry herbs.

- To release flavor oils from dried or fresh herbs, rub them briskly between fingers.

Garlic·

- To get the skins off garlic before chopping, pound each clove with the side of a heavy knife, meat pounder, or a bottle. The skin pops right off.
- Or soak garlic in warm water and the skin will peel off easily.
- To make fresh garlic salt: Cut or mash garlic on a board sprinkled with salt. The salt absorbs the juices. It also reduces the garlic odor. And garlic won't stick to the knife if you chop it with a little salt.

Ginger

- After cleaning fresh ginger root with a scouring pad, cut or chop it up, place in a screw-top jar, then immerse in dry sherry or vodka. This will keep for months in your refrigerator.
- Store ginger by burying it in moist soil or sand. It lasts for months and may even grow into a plant!

Herbs

- Make up herbed and other flavored butters (such as garlic and butter) for a quick sauce to add to a hot vegetable.
- A good idea for seasoning soups, stews, and sauces is to bundle herbs together in a small cheesecloth bag that can be easily removed before serving.

Mint

- When chopping mint, sprinkle a pinch of sugar over it. This will draw out the juices and make chopping easier.

Onion salt

- Make fresh onion salt instantly: Cut a slice from the top of the onion, sprinkle salt on its juice, and scrape with a knife.

Parsley

- You can grow parsley in your own kitchen by cutting a small sponge in half and sprinkling a few parsley seeds over the halves. Put the sponges on dishes on windowsill, making sure to keep them moist.

- Did you know that parsley lends its freshness to other herbs? Try mincing equal amounts of fresh parsley with such spices as dried dill, basil, marjoram, or rosemary. You'll taste the difference.
- Put fresh parsley on a cookie sheet in the oven and leave it with only a pilot light on for a few days to dry it out. Store in jars in a cool dry place.

Pepper
- A few peppercorns in your pepper shaker will keep holes from clogging and give ground pepper a fresh taste.

Rosemary
- As rosemary is a rather splintery spice, you may want to put it in a pepper grinder for grinding over foods.

Salt
- A salt shaker that delivers salt too fast can be easily remedied by plugging up some of the holes. Wash shaker to remove all salt, dry thoroughly, and use colorless fingernail polish to stop up the desired number of holes.
- To prevent clogging, keep five to ten grains of rice inside your shaker.
- Since most recipes call for both salt and pepper, keep a large shaker filled with a mixture of both. A good combination is three-quarters salt and one-quarter pepper.

When to add salt
- Soups and stews: Add early.
- Meats: Sprinkle just before taking off the stove.
- Vegetables: Cook in salted water.

Whole spices
- In slow-cooking dishes use whole spices, as they take longer to impart their flavor.

A common error
- Never keep spices close to a kitchen range—they lose their flavor and color. For best results, store in refrigerator or any other cool dry place.

The Best of
Helpful Kitchen Hints
for
Entertaining
and Holidays

Let Me Entertain You

Faking baking
- Before guests arrive, give your home that "What's bakin'?" fragrance. Sprinkle cinnamon and sugar in a tin pie pan and burn it slowly on the stove.

Candle tips
- Make candles drip-proof by soaking them in salt water (two tablespoons of salt per candle and just enough water to submerge).
- Candles burn more slowly and evenly with minimal dripping if you place them in the refrigerator for several hours before using.

Nature's own cups
- Use a large green pepper as a cup for dips. Cut off top, scrape pepper clean of ribs and seeds, then fill with sour cream or other dip.
- Slice cucumber in half lengthwise, scoop out seeds, salt, and drain. Then fill.
- Use halved and hollowed-out melon or orange as a cup to fill with cut fruit.

Keep it on ice
- Fill a large bowl with crushed ice and place a bowl of potato, shrimp, or fruit salad in the ice up to the rim. Add a little kosher or ice-cream salt to the ice to make it colder.
- Your ice bucket is insulated so it will keep foods either hot or cold. Use it as a serving dish.
- Keep ice from melting by putting dry ice underneath a container of regular ice.
- Freeze red and green maraschino cherries in ice cubes. Or cocktail onions, mint leaves, or green olives for martinis on the rocks.
- To keep a salad, dip, or beverage really chilled, first weight your salad bowl down inside a larger bowl filled with water and freeze. Then remove from freezer and fill empty center bowl. Your dish will keep its cool throughout the meal. NOTE: Use only temperature-resistant bowls in the freezer.

Serve without spillovers
- To prevent dishes and tumblers from sliding on a serving tray, place them on damp napkins.
- Or, for silver trays, use a sheet of plastic wrap.

It's fun to flambé
- Any dessert wine can be used to flambé. First heat the wine over a low flame until it starts to boil. Reserving a tablespoonful, pour the rest of the heated wine over the food. Then carefully ignite the tablespoon of hot wine and pour over the food to flambé it. If the original liquor in a flambé pan refuses to light, heat fresh liquor in a spoon, pour over food, and ignite.

The party's over
- Treat a red-wine spill on the rug with ordinary shaving cream from an aerosol can. Then sponge off with cold water. Always test on an out-of-sight area first.
- Or immediately cover the stain with a liberal amount of salt or baking soda. Leave until the stain is completely absorbed, then vacuum.
- Or remove with club soda.

- Remove white water rings from furniture with a soft, damp cloth and a dab of white toothpaste, then polish as usual. Make sure you always rub along the grain of the wood.
- Candle-wax drippings on cloth and carpets can be removed by placing a brown paper bag over the spot and running a hot iron over it.
- To repair a burn, remove some fuzz from the carpet, either by shaving or pulling out with a tweezer. Roll into the shape of the burn. Apply a good cement glue to the backing of the rug and press the fuzz down into the burned spot. Cover with a piece of cleansing tissue and place a heavy book on top. The fluff will dry very slowly and you'll get the best results.
- Smoke smells will quickly disappear when a cold wet towel (wrung out) is swished around the room.

Keep Up
the Holiday Spirit

A "cover-up" for New Year's Eve
- For an elegant New Year's Eve dinner party, use refrigerated Crescent dinner rolls as a quick and easy pastry to prepare a beef Wellington.

Have heart-shaped cake

- Make a heart for *your* Valentine: First bake both a round and a square cake. Cut round cake in half, then turn the square cake so the corners face you in a diamond shape. Place each half of the round cake on the two uppermost sides of the diamond. Now you have a perfect heart-shaped cake. Frost and serve.

The egg hunt is on

- Make your own Easter-egg dyes. Boil the eggs with grass for green, onion skins for yellow, and beets for red.

For April showers

- Color cream cheese with powdered or liquid vegetable coloring as a filling for dainty rolled sandwiches. Try a different color for each layer and slice as you would a jelly roll.
- For attractive individual butter servings, squeeze softened butter through a pastry bag or plastic bag onto a cookie sheet; set in refrigerator to harden.

Gobs of cobs

- For Fourth of July cookouts or other large parties you can grill corn, husk and all. First let cobs soak in water for an hour or so, then secure the ends with wire-twist ties, and place on grill, turning every ten minutes until done (about thirty to forty-five minutes).
- For hot, buttered corn, fill a large quart jar with hot water and sticks of butter. When butter melts and floats to top, dip in the cobs and pull out slowly. The butter covers the corn perfectly.

Keeping pumpkins very well

- To preserve Halloween pumpkins, just spray inside and outside surfaces with a spray-on antiseptic to kill bacteria and keep the pumpkin in shape.

A good measure of blessings

- To be sure your turkey's done, test your thermometer by placing it in boiling water. It should read 212°. If it doesn't, just add or subtract the difference from your reading while cooking. Remember to warm the thermometer in water before plunging it into poultry or meat, and for a more accurate reading keep it away from fat or bone.
- Keep your mashed potatoes hot simply by covering them with cotton or linen napkins and putting the cover back on the pot.

All the trimmings

- Sift a little cornstarch over hard Christmas candy when you put it in the dish. Stir. Candy will not stick together or to the dish.
- To restore a dried-out fruitcake, turn it upside down, poke a few holes, and drop in some frozen orange juice. The juice will melt slowly and spread throughout the cake instead of running right through. After the juice has melted, turn the cake over and the holes won't show.
- Keep fruitcakes fresh indefinitely by wrapping them in a damp towel. Dampen the towel with wine for a special flavor.

It is better to give
- For wrapping an extra-large gift, try a Christmas table-cloth made of paper. It's easy to handle and less expensive than several sheets of wrapping paper.
- For a last-minute gift, keep a best-selling cookbook available and quickly add an inscription.
- Wrap a current issue of a popular magazine and add a tag saying that a subscription is on the way.

Keeping and reusing cards
- Want to save special cards? Giving each card a coating of hair spray prevents the colors from fading.
- Reuse cards you receive for any occasion by putting a little household bleach on a cloth and rubbing gently over any handwriting.

"Choc" it up
- After holidays, shop for the half- and 1-pound solid chocolate bunnies, Santas, Valentines, etc., when they go on sale for half price. Cut up for excellent chocolate-chip cookies or a multitude of other chocolate uses and save more than double your money.

A bowl with punch
- Mix a wine punch in advance so ingredients blend better. To serve the punch fresh and bubbly, add well-chilled club soda just before serving.
- Melting ice cubes won't affect your party punch if you use cubes made by freezing a moderate amount of punch in ice-cube trays. Or fill small rubber balloons with water and freeze them. The colorful ice balloons will float. (Wash balloons well first.)
- For huge cubes to keep punch cold, fill washed milk cartons or salad molds with water and freeze them. When ice is partially frozen add fruit for a colorful touch. Remember, the larger the ice cube, the more slowly it melts.
- Poke peppermint sticks through the centers of orange or lemon slices and float them in your Christmas punch for a beautiful garnish.

Swizzle sticks you can eat
- Use long, thin slices of peeled cucumber for Bloody Marys.

- Make your own "dilly" beans by marinating fresh green beans in leftover pickle juice for martinis on the rocks.
- Use candy canes for eggnog drinks.

Vodka
- Vodka kept in the refrigerator is more flavorful. Pour over ice cubes of frozen tomato juice for a Bloody Mary on the rocks.
- To pour gin or vodka over vermouth-tinged ice cubes, first swirl ice in a few drops of dry vermouth, then empty all liquid from glass for the hard stuff.

Champagne
- Chill champagne bottle in ice bucket only up to the neck, or removing cork may be troublesome.
- If removing plastic cork is difficult, run hot water on the neck of the bottle. Heat expands the glass, causing the cork to pop out.
- Do not chill champagne in refrigerator for hours. Its flavor is more delicate if chilled for only a short while on ice.

Keeping wine well
- Wine from jugs that have been opened can be rebottled and its life extended by being poured into smaller wine bottles, but be sure to leave very little air space between wine and cork.

The Best of
Helpful Kitchen Hints
for
Outdoor
Barbecuing

Grill Work

Light my fire
- Pour enough briquettes into a grocery bag for one barbecue and fold it down. When you have a quantity of bags filled, pile one on top of the other until ready to barbecue. Then simply place one paper bag of briquettes in the barbecue and light. The charcoal will catch very quickly and you will have clean hands.
- Pack charcoal briquettes in egg cartons and tie shut. There's no mess and you can light them right in the carton in the barbecue.
- To get a quick blaze when you build a wood fire, soak an unglazed brick in kerosene for a day. The brick will start your fire immediately. It will ignite damp logs without kindling and burn for quite a while on the kerosene fuel alone.
- Add a delicious flavor to barbecuing by sprinkling the coals with fresh herbs that have been soaked in water first.

Fast action for flareups
- When flareups from fat drippings start to burn the meat, place lettuce leaves over the hot coals.
- Or keep a pan of water and a turkey baster next to the barbecue, and squirt water to put out flare-ups.
- Or, when flare-ups occur, simply space the coals farther apart and raise the grill.

On and off the grill
- Put the burger fresh from the grill into the bun and place the whole thing in a plastic bag for about a minute. The warmed bag becomes a wonderful steamer.
- Put on a few extra steaks and broil them over charcoal until partly done. Then freeze. At a later date, finish broiling them indoors for that outdoor taste.

Marination sensations
- To marinate meats easily, place in a plastic bag with sauce and seal tightly. Turning the bag just once coats all the pieces at the same time.

- To tenderize chicken or pork chops, boil them in a sauce-pan for fifteen minutes. Then drain and let marinate in barbecue sauce for thirty minutes. Now meat is ready to barbecue.

Fire tending
- To prevent burns when roasting hot dogs and marshmallows on a stick, cut a hole in the center of an old pie tin and slip the stick through. The pie tin shields the hand.
- Or, for other work near the fire, a canvas work glove soaked in water protects hands. NOTE: Never touch extremely hot objects with wet gloves.

Cut the cleanup
- Coat the bottoms of pots and pans with shaving cream or bar soap before cooking on open fire. The black marks come off without much scouring.
- Coat the grill with vegetable oil before cooking. Begin cleaning as soon as the grill is cool to the touch.
- Or wipe the grill with a piece of crumpled aluminum foil while it's still warm.
- Or spray a greasy grill while it's still warm with window cleaner.
- Or, using a thick kitchen mitt, wrap the grill in several layers of wet newspaper while it's still hot. It steams itself clean.

Blow-away insurance
- To prevent picnic tablecloths from blowing in the wind, sew pockets into the corners, putting old keys in each one to weight them down.

- Or put two-sided adhesive tape here and there on the table, especially the corners.
- Or try a fitted sheet for a junior-size bed. Most are the same size as the standard picnic table and fit the tabletop as they do a bed.
- Paper plates won't blow away if you use thumbtacks.

Cool ideas

- Melted paraffin wax, applied to the inside and outside of a cooler leak, will seal it.
- Use a sugar bag instead of a plastic bag for storing ice cubes because it's thicker and insulates better.
- Wrap a watermelon as soon as you take it from the refrigerator in burlap or dry newspaper. It should stay cool until ready to eat.

The Best of Helpful Kitchen Hints
for
Freezing

The Cold Facts

On your mark
- If you need a label in a hurry when freezing an item in aluminum foil, write food description on a plastic bandage, then peel off the backing and apply to foil.

Get set
- To freeze food in plastic bags, remove as much air as possible. Gather the tip of the bag around an inserted straw, suck out the air, then remove the straw and close the bag tightly.
- Freezing expands food and liquids, so always allow at least one-half inch of space at the top of the container before putting it in freezer.
- Most foods stick together when frozen, so flash-freeze them to eliminate this problem. Spread food on cookie sheet, freeze it, then remove and wrap in airtight containers before returning food to the freezer.
- Always scald or steam vegetables before freezing, as this prevents loss of color, texture, and flavor.

Everybody Freeze!

Bananas
- Run overripe bananas through a sieve or mash them, add a little lemon juice, and freeze. Perfect for later use in cakes and breads.
- Or freeze whole bananas that are on the verge of going bad. They make delicious popsicles.

Bacon
- Lay strips side by side on a piece of aluminum foil or waxed paper. Roll them up lengthwise so they don't touch each other and put the roll in the freezer in a plastic bag. The bacon can be cooked as soon as it is thawed out enough to unroll.
- Crumble those extra pieces of cooked bacon and freeze them. Use as toppings for baked potatoes.

Blueberries
- Freeze them in the basket they come in, unwashed. Wrap container in aluminum foil or plastic wrap. They will keep their color and shape.

Bread (stale)
- Cut into tiny cubes. Brush with melted butter and toast them in the oven for later use as croutons. Then pop them into the freezer.

Brown sugar
- It won't harden if stored in the freezer.

Butter
- Save wrappings from sticks of butter or margarine. Keep in the refrigerator in a plastic bag for future use in greasing baking utensils.
- Unsalted butter can be stored in the freezer indefinitely if it's wrapped and sealed airtight. Salted butter can be stored for a shorter period in its orginal container with no wrapping.

Cabbage
- Wash and dry a head of cabbage with paper toweling, then wrap in a plastic bag and freeze. When defrosted, the leaves are limp and easy to remove and handle. Perfect for stuffed cabbage—and you won't have the odor of boiled cabbage throughout the house.

Cheese
- Cheese that can be frozen includes processed, Swiss, Greek cheese, Cheddar, and even cream-cheese dips. If, after defrosting, the cream cheese appears grainy, whip it well.
- Parmesan and Romano grate quite easily when frozen.
- And fifteen minutes in the freezer makes soft cheese easier to grate.

Coffee
- Coffee beans and ground coffee stay fresh longer when kept in the refrigerator or freezer.

Cream
- Freeze in original cartons if there is a half-inch space at the top of the container.
- Heavy cream whips well if a few ice crystals remain after defrosting.
- Leftover whipped cream: Drop dollops of whipped cream on a cookie sheet, then flash-freeze before storing in plastic bags.

Crêpes
- Stack with waxed paper between them. Let cool and wrap in aluminum foil to freeze.

English muffins
- Separate muffin halves before freezing. Later they'll be easier to toast.

Eggs
- Freeze them whole or separated.
- Freeze whole eggs in ice-cube trays that have been sprayed with vegetable oil. Freeze as many eggs as there are sections in the tray. Beat eggs gently in a bowl and add three-quarters teaspoon of sugar and one-quarter teaspoon of salt for every six eggs. Set a divider in the tray and pour the eggs into it. When eggs are frozen, place them in plastic bags. Each cube will equal one egg.
- Egg whites freeze perfectly for up to one year. Two tablespoons of white equal one egg white.
- Before freezing egg yolks, mix them with a pinch of salt and sugar to prevent coagulation.

Fish

- Freeze in clean milk cartons full of water. When thawing fish, don't forget that the water makes a good fertilizer for your houseplants.

Flour

- Flour can be frozen. Stock up when it's on sale.

Green pepper, garlic, and onions

- Chop and freeze in plastic containers. Keep adding to or use as needed for soups, stews, sauces, etc.

Ginger root

- Peel and freeze whole. When needed, grate the frozen piece.

Hamburger patties

- Flash-freeze individually and stack in aluminum foil.

Herbs

- They're not going to look too attractive when defrosted, but their flavor will still be great.

Honey

- Flash-freeze in ice-cube trays. If the honey becomes granular, simply place cubes in a jar in boiling water.

Ice cream

- Sometimes ice cream that has been opened and returned to the freezer forms a waxlike film on the top. To prevent this, press a piece of waxed paper against the surface of the remaining ice cream and reseal the carton.

Lemon and orange rinds

- Freeze. Grate rinds when needed.

Marshmallows

- Flash-freeze—and no more stale marshmallows!

Pancakes, French toast, waffles
- Too many? Flash-freeze and, when needed, toast in toaster or heat in 375° oven and serve.

Pickles, pimentos, olives
- Condiments in partially filled jars freeze well in their own liquid.

Popcorn
- It should always be kept in the freezer. It stays fresh, and freezing helps eliminate "old maids" when you pop it.

Potatoes
- Leftover mashed potatoes: Make patties and coat with flour for potato pancakes. Flash-freeze, then store in plastic bags. Don't bother defrosting before frying them in oil.
- Leftover baked potatoes: Cut in half; scoop out and mash potato. Mix in sour cream, grated Cheddar cheese, chives, salt, and pepper. Return to shells, then freeze.

Potato chips
- Freshest when wrapped and stored in the freezer. They don't get soggy.

Prunes, raisins, dates
- Dried fruit in partially filled boxes maintains freshness if frozen.

Sauerkraut
- Ready-to-use "kraut" freezes well in its own juice.

Tomatoes
- Freeze leftovers for use in soups and stews. They'll be mushy, but that won't affect the taste.

The thaw
- To defrost meats fast and safely, place meat in its original wrap or foil in bowl of cool water to cover. Pour salt in water and on wrap. Cover with lid and let stand about one hour.
- To defrost frozen ground beef quickly, sprinkle it with the amount of salt you plan to use in cooking. Salt greatly speeds thawing.
- Or try defrosting in your dishwasher, set on the drying cycle.
- Thaw a turkey quickly in an ice chest or picnic cooler placed in the bathtub. Fill the cooler with cold water and change the water frequently.

Freezer-failure emergencies
- To be sure that refrigerator or freezer hasn't defrosted and refrozen while you're on vacation, put a few ice cubes in a plastic bag in the freezer before you leave. On your return, if you find the ice in any other shape but cubes, you'll know you've got problems.

You put these in the refrigerator?
- Keep plastic wrap in the refrigerator to prevent it from sticking to itself when handled.
- Batteries and film stay fresh longer when kept in the refrigerator.
- Hydrogen peroxide won't lose its fizzle if kept in the refrigerator.
- Put your damp ironables in the refrigerator. They won't mildew and will be ready to iron when you are.
- Keep Band-Aids in the refrigerator and their backing will peel off in a snap.

The Best of
Helpful Kitchen Hints
for
Children

All My Children

On the bottle

- Keep the bottom of an electric coffeepot filled with a few inches of water in baby's room and use as a bottle warmer for early-morning feedings.
- Keep extra formula on hand in the refrigerator to add to a bottle of too-hot formula. It's faster than trying to cool a bottle under a faucet.
- Instead of traveling with bottles of milk, which will spoil, carry powdered milk in the bottles in the right amount. Later, just add water and shake bottle.

For crying out loud

- Remove peel and seeds from an orange, divide it into sections, and wrap and put them in the freezer. Baby will be soothed by the coolness when teething and get vitamin C as well.
- Use brown sugar instead of honey in making teething cookies. Honey keeps the cookies too moist.
- Stale bagels and other kinds of hardened bread make perfect teething foods.

Going off the bottle

- If you have trouble weaning your tot, take the nipple off the baby bottle and start him drinking directly from his familiar container—the old bottle.
- Or put a straw in the bottle.

Get a grip on the problem

- If you have trouble unscrewing the lids on baby-food jars, punch a small hole in the top of the lid. The hole lets air out of the jar, and it can be easily opened. If any food is left over, cover the lid with aluminum foil and refrigerate jar.
- A couple of wide, colorful rubber bands wrapped around children's drinking glasses provide a steadier grip for tiny hands. A strip of adhesive tape can also help.

Cleanups

- Get rid of baby-food stains with this solution: one cup of bleach, one cup of dishwasher detergent, and two to three gallons of water. Let material soak a few hours before washing it.
- Also, try rubbing a paste of unflavored meat tenderizer on formula stains. Roll the clothes up and wait a few hours before washing them in the machine.
- To remove odor instantly from spit-ups, apply a paste of baking soda and water to the fabric.

Avoiding falls

- Attach to the back or side of baby's highchair a small-sized towel rack to hold all the things needed at mealtime (bib, washcloth, and towel).
- Prevent baby's highchair from tipping over by screwing a screen-door fastener to the wall. Attach the hook to the back of the highchair and latch the chair to the wall.
- Put a small rubber mat you would use in the sink on the seat of the highchair to keep baby from sliding out.

It's partytime

- Write the invitation on blown-up balloons with felt markers. Let them dry, then deflate. Then mail them to the children, who must blow up the balloon to read the invitation.
- Prepare your favorite cake mix according to directions. Fill ice-cream cones, the kind with flat bottoms, half full with cake batter and arrange on a cookie sheet. Bake at 350° for twenty minutes, cool, and add a scoop of ice cream.

- Use small marshmallows as candleholders for a birthday cake. They prevent the wax drippings from running into the frosting.
- To keep ice cream from leaking through the bottom of a cone, put a marshmallow in the bottom.

Painting the town
- Make fingerpaints in your kitchen by mixing two cups of cold water and one-quarter cup of cornstarch, then boil liquid until thick. Pour into smaller containers and color with various food colorings.
- For a great playdough for your children, mix one cup of salt and two cups of flour and add enough water to make a soft dough. Add any food coloring desired. Keep tightly sealed.
- Make colorful beads from cut macaroni by dunking them into assorted food colors. Drain and dry completely. Pour the beads into individual paper cups and let older children make their own necklaces.

These little kiddies went out to lunch

- Most sandwiches can be stored in the freezer for two weeks. Make them once every two weeks and save yourself a lot of time.
- To keep sandwiches from becoming limp and soggy, spread butter or margarine all the way to the crusts of the bread before adding filling.
- Here are a few suggestions for fillings that can be frozen: cold cuts, peanut butter (jelly does not freeze well), cheese, meat loaf and catsup, chicken, turkey, beef, and tuna-fish salad. (Mayonnaise can be frozen if the filling is no more than one-third of the sandwich volume.)
- To prevent frostbite, wrap sandwiches very securely in freezer paper or aluminum foil.
- Pack sandwiches in the lunchbox right from the freezer. They will thaw in time for lunch.
- Save small plastic pill containers with snap-on lids. They're great for holding salad dressings, catsup, or mustard.
- Make portable salt and pepper shakers by cutting straws, filling with salt and pepper, and twisting ends up.

This little kiddie stayed home

- Turn a Sloppy Joe into a "Tidy Joseph" by slicing a thin layer from the top of an unsliced hamburger bun. Scoop out enough bread to make a bowl. Fill with Sloppy Joe mixture. Replace the top slice and you now have a "Tidy Joseph."

Thermos thoughts

- Wrap a cooked hot dog in plastic and put it in a Thermos of hot soup or water. At lunchtime, the hot dog can be served in a bun. No more soggy buns!
- For a shrunken Thermos cork, boil the cork in a covered pot until it expands to fit the bottle again.
- To prevent the cork from souring in a Thermos, place a small piece of plastic wrap over the cork.
- To protect a Thermos bottle from breakage, cut the foot off a large old sock and slip it over the Thermos.

Choice "kid-bits"

- Sandy bottom: Bring along a playpen minus the floor. Set it on the beach or grass so young tots can play safely while you picnic.

- Brushups: Keep a minuteglass in the bathroom. Following meals, have your child brush until top of glass empties.
- On trays: Serve meals to a sick child in bed in a muffin tin. There are enough compartments for food and even a small drinking glass.
- Smooth sledding: A child's sled will go down the hill faster if you spray vegetable oil on the bottom. Works on inner tubes, too.

Getting gum off hair
- Rub on a dab of peanut butter. Massage the gum and peanut butter between your fingers until the gun is loosened. Remove it gently with a comb, then shampoo hair.

Making sharing easy
- If children argue over who gets the largest portion when sharing a treat, let one child divide the treat while the other selects his/her portion first.

Safety firsts
- Always turn the handles of pots and pans toward the inside of the stove to avoid their being knocked off by children.
- Keep your toddler out of kitchen cabinets by placing a yardstick through the handles of each cabinet drawer.
- Keep tablecloth edges folded up on top of the table so your toddler won't be able to pull them.
- Always keep dishware and utensils in the middle of the table of counter to keep them from falling on your child.
- Your tot will be able to tell the hot-water faucet from the cold one if you mark the hot with red tape.

The Best of
Helpful Kitchen Hints
for
Cleaning

Startin'
at the Bottom

Note: When using these hints, remember: Unplug any household appliance before cleaning it. Rinse and dry thoroughly any appliance, pot, or pan after cleaning and before using it again. Before using any of these hints on floors, carpets, fabrics, lineoleum, etc., always test first on a small corner or, if possible, on an out-of-sight area. Special care should always be taken in households with small children.

The kitchen carpet
- Instant spot removers:
    Prewash commercial sprays
    Glass cleaner
    Club soda
    Shaving cream
    Toothpaste
  Apply one of the above to the stained area. Rub it in and wait a few minutes before sponging it off thoroughly. If the stain is still present, combine two tablespoons of detergent, four tablespoons of white distilled vinegar, and one quart of warm water. Work into stain and blot, blot, blot.

Carpet brighteners
- Combine two cups of cornmeal and one cup of borax for an excellent carpet cleaner and deodorizer. Just sprinkle on and leave for one hour before vacuuming.
- Or sprinkle a generous amount of baking soda on the carpet before vacuuming.

A static and shock remover
- Mix one part liquid fabric softener with five parts water in a spray bottle. Mist the carpet very lightly. Let dry and you'll have no more clinging pet hairs or unwanted carpet fuzz on clothing.

A step saver
- Make your vacuuming easier by adding a thirty-foot heavy-duty extension cord to your sweeper cord.

Touch-ups
- Dingy, discolored carpet spots will disappear if indelible ink of the same color is rubbed in.

Sliding rugs
- Throw rugs will stay in one place if rubber canning rings are glued to the bottom.

The Linoleum

The best floor cleaner
- Combine one-half cup of bleach, one-quarter cup of white distilled vinegar, one-quarter cup of washing soda, and one gallon of warm water for the perfect solution for washing floors. (Do not use on cork.)
- If a mopped floor dries with a film that dulls the luster, pour one cup of white vinegar into a pail of water and go over the floor again.
- Before putting your mop away, soften it by dunking it in a fresh pail of water and a capful of fabric softener.

When you're out of floor wax
- Add one-half cup of vinegar and two tablespoons of furniture polish to a pail of warm water.
- Or add a capful of baby oil to detergent and water.
- Or add some skim milk to the wash water.

It's time to strip the old wax
- Try this solution: one cup of Tide laundry detergent, six ounces of ammonia, and one gallon of warm water.

Nonsticking tiles?
- No linoleum cement available and tiles won't stick to the floor? Apply a layer of denture cream to the back of the tiles. Put a few heavy books over the area and let dry for twenty-four hours.

Heel and crayon marks?
- Black heel marks and crayon marks can be removed by rubbing with a damp cloth and a dab of toothpaste.

Cleaning hard-to-reach places
- Slip a sock or two over the end of a yardstick and secure with a rubber band.
- Or staple a small sponge to the end of a yardstick to reach under the refrigerator and radiators.

Smooth move
- Glue pieces of old carpeting to the bottom of chair legs. The chair will slide more easily and won't leave marks on the floor.

Broken glass?
- To pick up shards of broken glass, mop the area with a piece of soft bread or damp paper toweling.

Movin' on Up

The best wall cleaner
- Combine one-half cup of ammonia, one-quarter cup of white vinegar, one-fourth cup of washing soda, and one gallon of warm water.

Start from the bottom
- Always begin washing walls at the bottom instead of the top and wash upward. Why? If dirty water runs down over soiled areas it leaves streaks that are harder to remove.

To remove everyday smudges
- Erase light marks with gum erasers (avilable at stationery and art-supply stores).
- Or rub the soiled areas with chunks of fresh bread.

Grease spots?
- Sprinkle white talcum on a clean powder puff. Rub the puff over the spot, repeating the process until the grease disappears.
- Or make a paste of cornstarch or fuller's earth and water. Let it remain on the spot for a few hours, then brush it off. If the stain is still present, try, try again.

Filling nail holes
- On wallpapered walls: All you need is a box of crayons. Soften the crayon tip over a match for a few seconds. Wipe it off with paper toweling before rubbing it into the hole. Two or more colors may have to be used to match unusual shades. Wait several minutes, then remove the excess color by rubbing gently with paper towels.
- On white walls: Patch with equal parts salt and starch. Add enough water for a smooth surface.
- Or fill hole with white toothpaste.
- On colored walls: Use one of the above methods but add food coloring to match wall color.
- On woodwork: Mix a little dry instant coffee with spackling paste or starch and water. Smooth with a damp cloth.

Is your screw loose?
- Instead of replacing the paper-towel holder because the screw hole in the wall has been stripped, saturate a cotton ball with Elmer's glue. Gently push the entire cotton ball into the hole. Allow it to dry at least twenty-four hours, then insert the screw gently with a screwdriver.

Disappearing paste-ups
- Hang posters and lightweight pictures on your kitchen walls with toothpaste. It's easy to clean off when you take the picture down, and you won't have unnecessary nail holes.

High-gloss paneling
- Add one cup of any type of time-saving floor wax to one gallon of water. Wash with a soft cloth. This solution helps guard against finger marks, too.

The Windows

The best window cleaner
- Add one-half cup of ammonia, one-half cup of white distilled vinegar, and two tablespoons of cornstarch to a bucket of warm water for a perfect window-washing solution.
- For fast cleanups, wash with a cloth soaked in white vinegar. Dry with crumpled newspapers.

More cleaners
- For stubborn spots, spray glass with oven cleaner. Leave it there for a few minutes before wiping grime away.
- Your windows will sparkle when washed with one quart of cold water and two capfuls of Woolite Cold Wash.
- During the winter, add denatured alcohol to water you use for cleaning windows to prevent freeze-ups.

Curtains

- Kitchen curtains will hold their body and require less ironing if one-half cup of Epsom salts is added to the final rinse water when washing.
- Preventing curtain ripoffs: Cut off the finger of an old glove to cover your curtain-rod end before slipping it through delicate curtains. Plastic bags work well, too.
- A foolproof way to get tiebacks straight across from each other when hanging curtains is to use your window shade as a measuring guide.

Round 'n' Round the Kitchen

The cupboards

- Cold tea is a good cleaning agent for woodwork of any kind.
- Renovate cupboards that have become faded in spots by rubbing and buffing shoe polish of the same color into the stained areas. Two or three different colors may be needed to accomplish the job.

To remove old contact paper

- Run a warm iron over the contact paper and it should peel right off.
- Instead of contact paper, try using floor tiles to line pantry shelves. They clean easily and last forever.

The counters

- To remove juice, coffee, or tea stains, scrub them vigorously with a paste of baking soda and water. Let set for half an hour, then wipe paste up with a wet sponge.
- Nicked Formica counter tops can be touched up with matching crayon or paint.

The oven

- An inexpensive oven cleaner: Set oven on warm for about twenty minutes, then turn it off. Place a small dish of full-strength ammonia on the top shelf. Put a large pan of boiling water on the bottom shelf and let it sit overnight. In the morning, stand back and open the oven. Let it air awhile before you wash it with soap and water. Even the hard, baked-on grease will wash off easily. For a badly stained oven, repeat the operation the next night. (Ammonia fumes are dangerous, so open the outside kitchen door before opening oven door. Do not use this hint in kitchens with inadequate ventilation.
- Put all the removable parts of your stove into a plastic garbage bag and pour in a couple of cups of ammonia. Seal the bag with a tie and leave outdoors for several hours. Rinse clean with the garden hose. No mess and no scrubbing. Try this trick to keep the chrome rings on electric ranges clean.
- Following an oven spill, sprinkle the area with salt immediately. When the oven is cool, brush off burned food and wipe with a damp sponge. Or sprinkle the oven bottom with automatic-dishwasher soap and cover with wet paper towels. Let this stand for a few hours.

Badly stained broiler pan

- Sprinkle the hot pan heavily with dishwasher detergent or dry laundry detergent. Cover with a dampened paper towel and let the burned food stand for a while.
- Or spray with oven cleaner.

The refrigerator

- Add a little baking soda to the soapy wash water to deodorize the inside of the refrigerator.
- To prevent mildew from forming, wipe refrigerator with vinegar. The acid effectively kills mildew fungi.

The freezer

- After the freezer has been defrosted, spray it with alcohol or vegetable-oil spray. The next time you defrost, it will take less work.
- Place a piece of waxed paper under your ice-cube trays and they will never stick to the bottom.

Automatic ice maker not working?

- When ice cubes freeze together and jam up ice maker, hold hair-dryer blower about eight inches from frozen mass until melted.

Butcher blocks

- To clean butcher blocks, cutting boards, and wooden rolling pins, wash, then dry with cloth, then cover with salt to draw moisture out of the wood. Treat with mineral oil to maintain surface.
- To remove gummy dough, sprinkle salt on a wet sponge and start rubbing.
- Scrape butcher blocks and pastry boards with a plastic windshield scraper. It's easier to use than a knife, and it won't mar the wood.

Everything
and the Kitchen Sink

All-purpose kitchen cleaners

- Try trisodium phosphate (TSP), available at paint and hardware stores. It's a fantastic cleaning agent. Follow directions carefully: If the mixture is too strong, it can remove paint.

The sink

- When water corrosion or mineral-deposit buildup is a problem, try Chrome-R-Tile, by Santeen Products. It's available at hardware stores.
- Or lay strips of paper toweling around faucets where lime has accumulated. Pour vinegar on the toweling and leave it alone for one hour. Lime deposits will soften and be easy to remove.
- For a sparkling-white porcelain sink, place paper towels across the bottom of sink and saturate with household bleach. Let sit for half an hour or so.
- Sprinkle cream of tartar on a damp cloth to clean porcelain surfaces. This method also removes rust.

- Sprinkle automatic-dishwasher crystals on a wet sponge and scrub. This also works well on bathtub rings.
- Use a cloth dampened with rubbing alcohol or white vinegar to remove water spots from stainless steel.
- Rub stainless-steel sinks with lighter fluid if rust marks appear. Wash sink and hands thoroughly.

Chrome
- To keep chrome gleaming, polish with a soft cloth saturated with rubbing alcohol.
- Or ammonia and hot water—this is terrific.
- Or rub with dry baking soda and a dry cloth.
- Nail-polish remover is excellent for cleaning chrome decorations and knobs, especially on stoves. Be sure that all units are off and rinse well with water.

Stained dish drainers and trays
- Clean by soaking in bleach and water.
- Coat rubber drainboard trays with a light film of furniture polish to prevent staining. It makes the tray easier to clean, too.

Dishes
- Save time and money by using the cheapest brand of dishwashing detergent available and add a few tablespoons of vinegar to the dishwater. The vinegar cuts the grease and leaves dishes sparkling clean.
- When out of liquid dishwashing detergent, use a mild shampoo.
- A large cup hook hung in the kitchen by the sink makes a very handy holder for rings, watches, and bracelets while you're doing dishes.

Rust-free soap pads
- Stop a partially used steel-wool soap pad from rusting by wrapping it very tightly in aluminum foil and stashing it in the freezer.

Want a clean sponge and dish towel every day?
- To add freshness to old sponges, soak them overnight in a bowl of bleach and rinse well in the morning.
- Or wash them in the dishwasher.
- You'll have a clean towel every day if you wrap your dirty towel around one of the wires on the top shelf of your dishwasher and run it through a cycle.

Cookware
and
Appliances

Blender

- If it cannot be taken apart to wash, fill part way with hot water and add a drop of detergent. Cover and turn it on for a few seconds. Rinse and drain dry.
- To lubricate blenders, egg beaters, and any other kitchen appliances with movable parts, use mineral oil. Salad oil may corrode the metal. Mineral oil is noncorrosive and, like salad oil, it doesn't harm food.

Grater

- When you have two or more things to grate for one dish, grate the softest one first. Then the firmer foods "clean" the openings in the grater.
- After grating cheese, clean the grater by rubbing it with a raw potato.
- Use a toothbrush to brush lemon rind, cheese, onion, or other particles out of the grater before washing it.

Meat grinder

- Before washing the grinder, run a piece of bread or a raw potato through it.

Percolator

- Fill the percolator with water, add five tablespoons of salt, insert the tube, and let perk for fifteen minutes. Restore luster to a percolator by boiling vinegar in it.
- Sprinkle some salt into the strainer and pour hot water over it. This procedure removes the coffee grounds that clog the strainer basket.

- To clean the vertical tube of a percolator, run a pipe cleaner through it.
- To clean glass coffeepots: Drop in five or six ice cubes and sprinkle with salt. Swish around until pot is clean.

Pot holders
- If sprayed heavily with spray starch, pot holders will stay clean longer.

Pots and pans
- Sprinkle burned pots liberally with baking soda, adding a few cups of water. Simmer on stove awhile and then let stand for a few hours. You can usually lift the burned portion right out of the pan.
- Stubborn black burn marks: Heat pan and spray with oven cleaner. Wait half an hour before scouring.
- Stubborn stains on no-stick cookware can be removed by boiling two tablespoons of baking soda, one-half cup of vinegar, and one cup of water in stained pan for fifteen minutes. Reseason pan with salad oil.
- Enamel-pot stains can be easily removed. When a dark brown stain develops, mix bleach with water and boil in the pot until the stain disappears.
- To make your stainless-steel pots shine like a mirror, add one-quarter cup of bleach to the bottom of your dishwasher at the beginning of the cycle.
- To clean the inside of an aluminum pot that has turned black, boil a solution of two teaspoons of cream of tartar and one quart of water in it for a few minutes.
- Or cook tomatoes. The acid in tomatoes will bring back the old sparkle.
- Never use strong soap or alkaline scouring powders. These products darken and discolor aluminum.

A hint that takes the caking— off!
- Drop used fabric-softener pads (the kind you use in your dryer) into cooking utensils caked with baked-on food. Fill with water and let stand for one hour.

Cast-iron skillets
- Boil a little vinegar and salt in an iron skillet and watch the black spots and charred food disappear.
- Clean the outside of the pan with oven cleaner. Let it stand for an hour; the accumulated black stains can then be removed with vinegar and water.
- After washing and towel-drying, place the skillet in a warm oven to complete drying. Moisture is a skillet's worst enemy.
- Or, when it is clean, rub a small amount of oil on the inside of the pan to keep it seasoned.
- If rust spots appear, apply salad oil and allow to stand before wiping thoroughly. If rust spots do not disappear, try the same procedure again.
- Always place paper towels between cast-iron pans when stacking them.

Stainless-steel knives
- To get rid of black spots on steel knives, sprinkle some cleanser on the blade and wet an old wine-bottle cork. Scrub both sides of the knife with the flat end of the cork until the metal is clean.
- To keep stainless steel shiny and bright, rub with a piece of lemon peel, then wash in sudsy water.
- Or use rubbing alcohol.

Teakettle
- To remove lime deposits, fill the kettle with equal parts of vinegar and water. Bring to a boil and allow to stand overnight.
- Or fill with water and refrigerate for about half a day. The lime is worked free by the cold and will come out when the kettle is emptied.
- For Corningware teapots, fill with water and drop in two denture-cleaning tablets. Let stand thirty minutes and rinse well.
- Or pour one-quarter cup of vinegar or lemon juice in the pot and fill with hot water. Let stand a couple of hours and rinse.

Toasters

- Shine up with club soda or a little ammonia and lots of water.
- Use lighter fluid or nail-polish remover to remove plastic that has burned on the toaster and any other electrical appliance.

Waffle iron

- Use a toothbrush to spread oil around waffle iron. When you're finished using the iron, use the same brush to scrub between the rows with soapy water.

Pampering
the Valuables

Brass

- Mix equal parts of salt and flour and add a little vinegar to make a paste. Spread a thick layer on the brass and let it dry. Rinse and wipe off paste.
- Or use toothpaste or very fine steel wool dipped in furniture polish.

China

- Before washing fine china and crystal, place a towel on the bottom of the sink to act as a cushion.
- To remove coffee or tea stains and cigarette burns, rub spot with a damp cloth dipped in baking soda.
- Wash plate in warm water, a mild detergent, and one-quarter cup of ammonia. Rinse it very thoroughly.

Copper

- Fill a spray bottle with hot vinegar and add three tablespoons of salt. Spray solution liberally on copper pots. Let sit for a while, then rub it clean.
- Or try lemon juice and salt.

Glass

- Never use your dishwasher or hot water for washing fine glass, especially when it is gold-rimmed.
- Never put a delicate glass in water bottom side first; it can crack from sudden expansion. The most delicate glassware is safe if slipped in edgewise.
- Keep crystal shining by washing in a sinkful of warm water and one-quarter cup of ammonia.
- White distilled vinegar is a must for rinsing crystal. Add one cup of vinegar to a sinkful of warm water.
- Dry with completely dry towels.
- Or try a chamois. It eliminates all lime and water spots, and polishes windows and mirrors, too.

Glass troubles

- When fine crystal stains or discolors, fill glasses with water and drop a denture tablet in. Let stand until discoloration disappears.
- Or mix sand with denatured alcohol and swish it around the glass until the cloudiness is gone.
- Clean vases with narrow necks by dampening the inside of the vase with water and adding toilet-bowl cleanser. Let stand for ten minutes and stains will disappear.
- Or fill with hot water and add two teaspoons of vinegar plus some rice and shake well.
- Or, to clean a glass decanter, chop and dice a large potato into small pieces, put it into the decanter with some warm water, and shake rapidly.

Pewter

- To clean *old pewter*, use a mild kitchen scouring powder moistened with olive oil. For a very stubborn stain, dip very fine steel wool in water or kerosene and rub gently. Rinse with soap and water.
- Today's *new pewter* requires a minimum of cleaning because it is made from a tarnish-proof alloy. It can be cleaned by washing with soap and water.
- Or try a homemade mixture of wood ashes moistened with water on both new and old pewter.

Silver

- Here's an amazing time saver for polishing tarnished silver: Line the bottom of a pan with a sheet of aluminum foil or use an aluminum pan. Add three tablespoons of baking soda or Spic and Span or Soilax to each quart of water used. Heat the water to almost boiling. Dip the silver into the water and let it remain until the tarnish disappears. The silver must touch the aluminum.
- When using silver polish, add a few drops of ammonia and watch the results.
- If polishing only a few pieces, try toothpaste.
- Make sure silver is dry before putting it away. It's best to leave out for several hours after polishing or washing. Dampness can cause silver to rust, which appears as black spots.

Do's

- Do wash silver as soon as possible after it's had contact with eggs, olives, salad dressings, vinegar, and foods heavily seasoned with salt. These foods, especially eggs and salt, cause silver to tarnish rapidly.
- Do place a piece of chalk in silver chest to absorb moisture and prevent tarnishing.
- Do buy silvercloth, the tarnish-retardant flannel, available at better fabric stores, and make your own bags for storing silver. You'll save those extra dollars.

Don'ts

- Don't store plated silver in newspaper. Printer's ink can remove the plating.
- Don't use rubber gloves when polishing silver or fasten silver with rubber bands or place near rubber—rubber darkens silver.

Nose Encounters
of the Worst Kind

Refrigerator and freezer odors
- Pour one of the following "odor eaters" into a saucer and place it in your refrigerator: charcoal, dried coffee grounds, vanilla bean or extract on a piece of cotton, baking soda, or crumpled newspaper.

For odors that won't go away
- When all else fails, place a coffee can full of charcoal on the refrigerator shelf and leave it for a few days. Repeat until odor is gone.
- Also make a paste of baking soda and water and spread it all over the inside of the refrigerator. Use cotton swabs to ensure that you get every corner and crevice. Wait a few days before sponging off.
- And make sure the drain pan on the bottom of the refrigerator is clean.

Drain away odors
- Once a week, pour one-quarter of a mixture of one cup of baking soda, one cup of salt, and one-quarter cup of cream of tartar down the drain. Follow with a pot of boiling water, then flush with cold water. This helps keep drains open and free of odors.

Cats and dogs on the go
- To get rid of odors from pet accidents, blot the area with paper towels, getting up as much of the mess as possible. Then shampoo the kitchen carpet or mop the floor with a strong solution of Massengill douche liquid. Carpets may need a few applications.

The nose "no's"
- Eliminate odor in shoes by shaking a little baking soda in them.
- Use baking soda as an odorless deodorant.
- For sweet breath, chew parsley.

Cover-ups
- When the trash compactor is running to full capacity, a few drops of oil of wintergreen will reduce odors.
- Before vacuuming, saturate a cotton ball with lemon juice or oil of wintergreen and place it in vacuum-cleaner bag or canister to deodorize air as you go.
- Add a drop of cologne or air freshener to the wheel of your humidifier. The fragrance will spread throughout the house.
- After cleaning an oven, eliminate the lingering smell by baking orange peels in a 350° oven.
- Lighted candles will help keep rooms free of cigarette smoke.

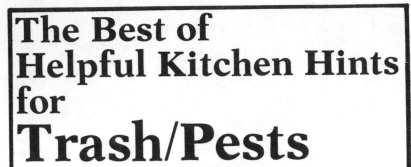

The Best of
Helpful Kitchen Hints
for
Trash/Pests

Getting the Bugs Out

Bugging off
- Throw a few mothballs in the garbage can to neutralize odors and keep out insects.
- Or sprinkle ammonia around trash cans to keep dogs and pests away.

Downright upright
- Place outdoor garbage can inside an old car tire for a firm anchor.

Roaches take a powder
NOTE: These hints are not for use in homes with small children and/or pets.
- Sprinkle boric-acid powder or borax along baseboards in closets, under sink, refrigerator, stove, etc. Repeat every six months.
- Mix four tablespoons of borax, four tablespoons of flour, and one tablespoon of cocoa. Put mixture in jar lids or bottle caps and place them wherever roaches run.
- Fill a large bowl with cheap wine and set it under the sink. The roaches will drink it, get drunk, fall in it, then drown. This is not a joke. Its been known to have great results.
- Or place a bowl of dry cement and a bowl of water next to each other . . . and guess what happens.

Don't Mickey Mouse around
- Mice can't stand the smell of fresh peppermint. Put the sprigs in mouse-haunted places or saturate a piece of cardboard with oil of peppermint, available at most drugstores.
- If mint is hard to obtain, try trapping mice with a piece of cotton soaked in lard or bacon grease. Mice like to eat lard, and they like the cotton for their nests. Tack the cotton to the bait pan of the trap.
- Another good mousetrap bait is peanut butter. It usually works better than cheese.

Keep insects at bay

- Several bay leaves in a cupboard that has been thoroughly scrubbed are particularly effective against pests of all kinds. The leaves last about a year.
- Or sprinkle insect powder on a slice of raw potato and put it in a spot frequented by pests.

Worm squirms

- A few sticks of *wrapped* spearmint chewing gum placed on the shelf near open packages of noodles, macaroni, or spaghetti keep mealworms at a distance.
- A slice of raw potato in soil surface of potted plants draws out worms that could damage them.

Ant agonizers

- To keep ants out of the house, place whole cloves where they enter. And tuck a few in the corners of your kitchen cupboards and under the kitchen sink.
- Ants are never supposed to cross a chalk line. Draw a chalk line on the floor or wherever ants tend to march and see for yourself.
- Ants are also deterred by dried coffee grounds sprinkled around outside doors leading to the kitchen.
- For a lethal ant concoction, mix two cups of borax and one cup of sugar in a quart jar. Punch holes in the lid and sprinkle around the outside foundation of the house.

The sting

- Treat insect bites with a poultice of cornstarch or baking soda mixed with vinegar, fresh lemon juice, or witch hazel.
- Or try the white of an egg to relieve itching.
- Or rub the area with the juice from a broken rhubarb stalk.

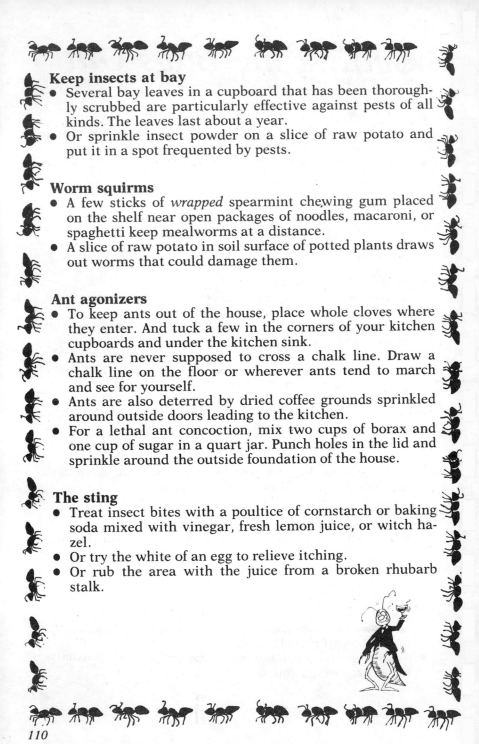

The Best of
Helpful Kitchen Hints for
Making Do

Using Something Else

Basting syringe
- Use to water small terrariums.

Cutting board
- For a good cutting board that can be taken anywhere, cover a thick magazine or several layers of cardboard with heavy-duty aluminum foil. It can also double as a hot pad.

Eyeglass case from the kitchen
- Make an inexpensive glasses case from a square pot holder. Just fold it in half and sew the bottom side. If you leave the loop on, you can keep reading glasses on a hook near where you cook.

Flour duster
- Keep a powder puff in your flour container. It's excellent for dusting flour on rolling pins, pastry boards, and other surfaces.

Funnel
- Make an instant funnel for dry substances such as sugar, salt, or flour by clipping the corner from an envelope or paper bag.
- For liquids: Clip the corners from a plastic bag or the fingertip of a rubber glove.
- Or use your gravy boat.
- Or cut a detergent bottle in half and clean it thoroughly.

Ice scraper
- Scrape ice from car windows with a Teflon spatula. It won't scratch the windows.

Measuring cup
- Use an ice-cream scoop; the average one holds exactly one-third cup.

Oyster and clam opener
- Use a beer-can opener to open oysters. Insert the point under the hinge at the top of the oyster and push down hard.

Rack or counter space
- Slide out a refrigerator shelf and use it as a cooling rack if you're baking a lot of cakes or bread.
- Or cool a pie or cake on a gas-burner grate.
- Create extra counter space when doing a lot of baking. Pull out a drawer or two and place a cookie sheet or tray across the top.

Rolling pin
- Use a wine bottle, filled with cold water and recorked, as a quick and efficient rolling pin.
- Or a cold bottle of soda pop wrapped in a stocking.

A ruler
- A dollar bill (or any other U.S. paper money) makes a handy measuring guide. Every bill is six and a quarter inches long.

Steamer
- If you don't have a steamer, improvise: Set a round strainer into a pan deep enough to hold several inches of water. The water level should be just below the strainer so that it doesn't touch or boil into it. You're ready to steam.

New twists for old problems
- Keep bread twist closures in your purse to attach buttons that might come off. Push through button's holes and twist closed on inside.
- Or temporarily repair with a twist eyeglasses from which the small screw is lost.

Using It All

...BUT WATCH WHERE YOU'RE SWINGING!

Last drops of catsup
- To get the last drops out of almost any catsup bottle, grab the bottom of the bottle and start swinging in a circular motion from your side. Just make sure you have the cap on tightly. The remaining drops will be forced to the top of the bottle.

Left with crumbs
- Keep a jar handy to store the leftover crumbs from empty boxes of cereals, crackers, or bread.

Sour wine
- Use it in place of vinegar, especially in marinades.

Flat club soda

- Don't throw away your fizzless club soda. It has just the right chemicals to add vigor and color to your plants.

Milk cartons

- They are free kindling. Start your fires with them. The same goes for candle stubs.

Egg cartons

- These serve as excellent storage containers for jewelry.

Eggshells

- Dry them in the oven and pulverize in the blender to make bonemeal, which is a good plant fertilizer.

Dried-out coconut

- Sprinkle with milk and let it stand until it regains its freshness.

Dried-out dates, figs, and raisins

- Steam in a strainer over hot water.
- Or place in a jar and sprinkle a little water over them. Set in refrigerator for a short time.
- Or heat in a 350° oven for a few minutes.

Crystallized jelly, honey, and syrups

- Set the bottle in a pan of hot water. Heat on stove until crystals disappear.

The last of the jelly

- Heat the jar in a pan of hot water and use the jelly to top waffles or pancakes.

Cardboard tubes

- Extension cords can be conveniently stored without tangling if you wind the cord loosely and slip it into a cardboard tube (from paper toweling or toilet tissue).

The energy crisis
- Use your pilot light in a gas range as a home food dehydrator. Lay chopped food you want to dry (celery, apples, onions, etc.) on foil and put in broiler oven on rack for about twenty-four hours. Store dry food in tightly closed containers. Buzz dried onions or garlic in blender to powder.
- Place small amounts of leftovers wrapped in aluminum foil in a large frying pan in one inch of boiling water. Cover and heat. Only one burner is used, and there are no extra pots to wash.

Teach
an
Old Bag
New Tricks

For shaking
- Place freshly made French-fried potatoes in a paper bag, add salt, and shake. In one easy motion the excess grease is absorbed and the potatoes are salted.

For keeping fresh
- To keep mushrooms from becoming slimy, always refrigerate them in a brown paper bag—never plastic. Paper lets the mushrooms breathe while holding in the humidity that keeps them fresh.

For storing
- Lettuce and celery will keep longer if you store them in the refrigerator in paper bags instead of cellophane. Do not remove the outside leaves until ready to use.

For draining

- To drain fat from foods, cover two paper bags with one sheet of paper toweling. Newspaper works also.

For baking

- When baking a pie, put it in an oven browning bag or a plain paper bag. Cut four or five slits in the bag and twist shut. Place on a cookie sheet and bake ten minutes longer than required time. Crust will turn a beautiful golden brown, and oven spills are eliminated.

Re-news for Nylons

For cleaning

- To clean kitchen drawers without removing the contents, cover your vacuum-cleaner nozzle with panty hose or cheesecloth and fasten with a rubber band.
- Cut the foot off an old nylon stocking, roll it up, and use it with cleansers for cleaning sinks without scratching.

For straining

- Use a clean, discarded nylon instead of cheesecloth for any straining jobs.
- Attach a used nylon stocking to the drain hose leading from your washing machine to shortstop lint that can clog the drain.

For finding

- Covering the vacuum-cleaner nozzle with panty hose and fastening with a rubber band is also a great way to pick up a contact lens lost in the carpeting.

For storing

- Store onions or potatoes in old nylon stockings so air can circulate around them and they'll last longer. Hang inside the kitchen closet.

For tying
- Use old nylons to tie up garbage bags, trees, plants, and shrubs, as well as old newspapers.

For dying
- Two similar stockings of different shades can easily be made into a matching pair. Drop them into boiling water and add a couple of tea bags. Remove them when the water has cooled and they will match perfectly. The more tea bags you use, the darker the shade will be.

Speedy Res-cubes

For household help
- To raise the nap of carpeting after heavy furniture has crushed it, place one or two ice cubes on the area. The next day, the cubes will have melted and the nap will be high.
- Ice cubes help to sharpen garbage-disposal blades.

For aches and pains
- Apply an ice cube immediately to lessen swelling and discoloration of a bruise.
- Or use to numb the area where a splinter has to be removed. This reduces pain.
- Make an instant ice bag by filling a zip-lock plastic bag with ice, placing a towel over bag, and beating ice with a hammer to crush.
- Hold an ice cube in your mouth to desensitize your taste buds before swallowing bitter medicine.

For ice-cube trays
- Ice-cube trays won't stick to the freezer compartment when a rubber fruit-jar ring or waxed paper is placed under the tray.
- Ice cubes won't stick to metal trays as much if the trays are oiled as you would a new frying pan. Coat them, wait a day, then wash with mild soap and warm water.

For crystal-clear cubes

- Boil water first, then chill in refrigerator and freeze. Did you know that boiling water makes ice cubes faster than cold because there is less oxygen in the water?

For cool-downs

- Use an ice cube to cool off children's soup so they don't burn their tongue. Tell them to stir it through the hot soup and that when it is melted, the soup is ready to eat.

The Best of Helpful Kitchen Hints for When Something Goes Wrong

Too Much

Too salty
- To soup or stew, add cut raw potatoes and discard once they've cooked and absorbed the salt.
- Or add sugar.
- Desalt anchovies by soaking them in cool water for fifteen minutes. Remove and pat dry with a paper towel.

Too sweet
- Add salt.
- Or add a teaspoon of cider vinegar.

Too much garlic
- Place parsley flakes in a tea ball and set it in the stew or soup pot until it soaks up the excess garlic.

Too sour-kraut
- When sauerkraut is too sour, drain and soak it in a large pot of cold water for ten minutes. Stir a little and drain.

Too much mayo
- If you slip and put in too much mayonnaise when making tuna salad and don't have another can of tuna to add to it, add some bread crumbs.

It's a Scorcher

Burned food
- Remove the pan from the stove immediately and set it in cold water for fifteen minutes to stop the cooking process. Then, with a wooden spoon, carefully remove the unburned food to another pan. Don't scrape, and don't include any pieces with burned spots unless they have been trimmed.

Meats
- Soak a towel in hot water and wring it out. Cover meat with it and let stand for five minutes before scraping off burned crust with a knife.

Milk
- Remove the burned taste from scorched milk by putting the pan in cold water and adding a pinch (one-eighth teaspoon) of salt.
- A small amount of sugar added but not stirred will help prevent milk from scorching.
- For easier cleaning, always rinse a pan in cold water before scalding milk in it.

Cake
- Let it cool before scraping off the burned layer with a knife. Frost with a thin coating of very soft frosting to set crumbs. Then cover with another thicker layer.

Biscuits
- Use a grater rather than a knife to scrape the bottom of burned biscuits. If you use a knife, you may end up holding a handful of crumbs.

Rice
- To remove the burned flavor from rice, place a piece of fresh white bread, preferably the heel, on top of the rice and cover the pot. In minutes the bad taste should disappear.

Gravy
- Add a teaspoon of peanut butter to cover up the burned flavor.

Butter or margarine
- Pour it over vegetables the way the French do, or use it for frying eggs.

It's Sticking

Unmolding the gelatin
- Soak a towel in hot water, wring it out, and wrap it around the mold for about fifteen seconds. Then, with both hands, unmold with a quick downward snap of the wrists. .

Pasta
- If drained pasta is glued together, reboil it another minute or so.

Fried foods
- When fried foods such as hash browns stick, place the pan on the cold surface of the bottom of the sink or in a large pan of cold water. Slide a spatula under the contents of the pan and everything slides right out. You even save the crusty bottoms this way.

Pastry dough
- If it sticks to the rolling pin, slip a child's sock (with the foot cut off) over it and sprinkle with flour.
- Or place the rolling pin in the freezer until chilled before flouring.

Cakes and cookies
- When a cake has cooled and is stuck to the pan, reheat cake in oven briefly. Still not loose? Place a damp towel on pan and let stand awhile.

It's Curdling

Mayonnaise
- Start over with another egg yolk and add the curdled mayonnaise drop by drop.

Hollandaise
- Remove sauce from heat and beat in one teaspoon of hot water, a few drops at a time. Do not return to heat. Serve warm or at room temperature.
- Or put hollandaise in saucepan over hot water in a double boiler. Add sour cream by the teaspoonful until the sauce is smooth.

Egg custard
- Slightly curdled egg custard can be restored by putting it into a jar and shaking hard.

Butter sauce
- If butter sauce is ruined by curdled yolks, keep heating it until the yolks release most of the butter. Strain out the butter and start over with fresh yolks, using the same butter.

The Best of Helpful Kitchen Hints for ...
Believe It or Not

Look What Things from the Kitchen Can Do!

Ammonia
- To remove a cork from the inside of a beautiful empty wine bottle, pour some ammonia into the bottle and set in a well-ventilated spot. The cork will disintegrate in a few days.

Bread
- A slice of bread will often remove makeup smudges from dark clothes.

Chili sauce
- Cats hate the smell of chili sauce! If your cat is climbing and scratching woodwork, just rub the area with chili sauce, buff off thoroughly, and your cat will stay clear! (Use this hint only for dark woodwork.)

Coke
- Along with detergent, add a bottle of Coke to a load of greasy work clothes. It will help loosen serious grease stains.
- Battery-terminal corrosion can be prevented by saturating each terminal with a carbonated drink.
- Instead of throwing leftover Coke down the kitchen drain, dump it down the toilet bowl and watch what happens. After it has soaked awhile, the toilet bowl should be sparkling clean.

Flour
- Clean white kid gloves by rubbing plain flour into the leather and brushing the dirt away.
- To clean plastic playing cards, drop the deck into a paper bag and add a few tablespoons of flour. Shake briskly, then wipe completely clean.

Karo syrup

- Grass stains can be removed from clothing by pouring a little Karo syrup on the stain. Rub fabric lightly, toss it into the washing machine, and the grass stain should wash away.

Kool-Aid and Tang

- Clean an electric coffeepot with Kool Aid. Run it through entire cycle, then rinse and dry it thoroughly.
- Clean the inside of your dishwasher by filling the dishwasher cup with Tang (the orange drink) instead of detergent. Wash without dirty dishes and run it through a complete cycle.

Lard

- If nothing else has worked to remove a grease spot from a solid-colored dress, try this—but only if you feel you have nothing to lose. Work lard through the material, covering every part of the spot evenly. Wash the garment thoroughly in hot suds and rinse well. The spot should have disappeared.

Lemon extract

- Will remove black scuff marks from luggage.

Milk

- Stains from ballpoint pens can be removed by sponging the area with milk until stain disappears.
- Red-wine stains on linen can be removed by immediately putting the material into a pot containing enough milk to cover the stained area. Bring to a boil and remove from burner. Let stand until the stain has completely disappeared. This method should also work on older wine stains.
- A simple way to remove cracks in china cups is to simmer the cup in milk for thirty to forty-five minutes, depending on the size of the crack. If the crack is not too wide, the protein in the milk will seal it.

Onions

- Light scorch stains on linen can sometimes be removed by rubbing the cut side of an onion over the stain. Then soak material in cold water.

Oven

- Have your tennis balls lost their bounce? If so, place the can of balls with the lid off overnight in a closed oven. The heat from the pilot light will get them back into shape.

Rice

- When postage stamps won't stick to the envelope, apply a few grains of cooked rice or some evaporated milk as a good emergency substitute for glue.

Salt

- A handful of salt in the washday rinse water will help keep clothes from sticking or freezing to the clothesline on damp, cold days.

Spoons

- To banish onion, garlic, and bleach odors from hands, put all five fingers on the handle of a stainless-steel spoon and run cold water over fingers.

Spaghetti

- To light candles in tall, deep containers, use a lit uncooked piece of spaghetti.

Tomato juice

- Help banish the odor from a new hair permanent. Apply enough juice to saturate dry, unwashed hair. Cover hair with a plastic bag and wait fifteen minutes. Rinse hair a few times before shampooing thoroughly.

Vegetable-oil spray

- Before cutting tall, damp grass, spray the cutting blade of the lawn mower with vegetable-oil spray and wet grass won't stick.

And Two More Amazing Hints

- If you have a cast-iron skillet without wooden handles that is encrusted with hard, baked-on outside grease, clean it by putting the pan in the fire in your fireplace. Let it get red for an hour or so. When it has cooled off, wash off soot with soapy water, then dry and oil it. It'll come out clean as a whistle.
- To prevent drinking glasses from cracking when filled with hot liquids (coffee, hot chocolate, etc.), place new glasses in a large pot. Fill the pot with cold water so the water covers the glasses entirely. *Slowly* bring the water to a boil. Turn the heat off and let the water cool. The glasses will never crack from hot beverages.

More hints to remember

Index

74; *grilling techniques,* 74–75; *for corn-on-cob,* 69; *tending fire,* 75; *wind protection,* 75–76

Basting syringe for watering, 112

Bathtub rings, 99

Batter tips, 44

Battery-terminal corrosion, 126

Bay leaves: *to drive out cupboard insects,* 110; *removing from stew,* 62 •

Beans, 17

Beating egg whites, 25

Beef roasts, 29; *pan juices,* 12, 29; *pan to use,* 29; *slicing of,* 29

Beef stock, 12

Beef Wellington pastry, 68

Beets, 17

Berries: *freshness test,* 57; *frozen, for cakes,* 44; *separation and hulling,* 57. *See also* Blueberries

Beverages, 37–39. *See also* names of beverages

Birthday candles: *lighting of,* 47; *marshmallow holders,* 87

Biscuits: *dough flakiness,* 42; *grating burned bottoms,* 122

Bleach, household: *cleaning with,* 99; *for deodorizing hands,* 129

Blender: *cleaning and lubrication,* 100; *uses:* creamy salad dressings, 14; delumping gravy, 30; pureéing vegetables for soup, 12; thawing frozen juice, 39

Bloody Mary: *and cucumber swizzle stick,* 71; *with tomato juice ice-cubes,* 72

Blueberries, 79

Blue cheese, 15

Boilovers: *prevention of,* 23, 36

Bonemeal: *from eggshells,* 115

Bones, 12

Borax: *for ants and roaches,* 109; *to clean and deodorize carpets,* 91

Brass cleaning, 103

Bread: *for burned rice,* 122; *to keep cake fresh,* 46; *as cleaning agent:* makeup on clothing, 126; smudges on walls, 94; to degrease pork chops, 29; with garlic for lamb roast, 29; to soak up fat in broiler pan, 39; *stale:* for broccoli and cabbage odor, 17; for croutons, 79; as teething food, 85

Bread-baking tips, 42–43

Bread crumbs: *storing of,* 114; *in tuna salad,* 121

Bread twist closures, 113

Briquettes. *See* Charcoal briquettes

Broccoli, 17

Broiler pan cleaning, 97

Broiling tips: *bacon and sausages,* 27; *safety rules,* 39–40; *steaks,* 29

Broken glass, 93

Broth. *See* Soups and broth

Brown sugar: *breaking up of lumps,* 51; *freezer storage,* 79; *for teething cookies,* 85

Bugs. *See* Insects

Buns: *sogginess in lunchbox,* 88; *stale, for salad toppings,* 15; *unwrinkling of,* 43

Burgers: *cooking for crowd,* 28; *outdoor grilling,* 74; *patties: defrosting of,* 83; *freezing of,* 81; *rounder and juicier,* 27

Burned food, 40, 121–123

Burned plastic on appliances, 103

Burned pots, 101

Burns, prevention of: *when barbecuing,* 75; *when broiling and steaming,* 39

Butcher blocks, 98

Butter(s): *when burned,* 123; *to soften cheese,* 26; *for corn on cob,* 69; *freezing of,* 79; *herb, as seasoning,* 63; *individual servings,* 69; *greasing pans with wrappings,* 79; *to remove skin from sauces and jellies,* 53

Buttermilk, 26

Butter sauce curdling, 124

Buttons: *reattachment of,* 113

Cabbage: *cooking odors,* 17–18; *hidden bugs,* 23; *freezing of, for stuffed recipe,* 79; *removing leaves from,* 17. *See also* Red cabbage

Café mocha, 38

Cake pans, 44–45, 123

Cakes, 44–46; *Angel-food,* 46; *adding bananas,* 46; *batter and flour to use,* 44; *when burned,* 122; *Cheese, defrosting of,* 46; *Chocolate,* 44, 46; *cutting and serving of,* 46; *decorating,* 47; *flavoring,* 46; *freezing and storing,* 46; *Fruit,* 70; *adding fruit and nuts,* 44; *heart-shaped for Valentine's Day,* 69; *Sponge, with orange juice,* 46; *when stale,* 46; *testing for doneness,* 46. *See also* Cake pans; Icings and frostings

cakes and waffles, 54, 115; Strawberry Glaze, 54. *See also* Icings and frostings
Tortillas, 32
Trays: *for extra counter space,* 113; *drainboard,* 99; *muffin tins as,* 89; *preventing spillovers,* 67
Trisodium phosphate (TSP), 98
Tuna salad, 121
Turkey, 32–33; *defrosting of,* 83; *testing for doneness,* 70

Vacuuming: *deodorizer for,* 107; *made easier,* 91; *and finding small items,* 117; *of kitchen drawers,* 117
Valentine's Day cake, 69
Veal bones, 12
Vegetable-oil spray: *for freezer defrosting,* 97; *for lawn mower blades,* 129
Vegetables, 16–23; *boilovers,* 23; *and bugs,* 23; *with burned butter,* 123; *and color fading,* 17, 23; *cooking two in foil,* 23; *freezing of leftovers,* 12; *frozen, restoring of flavor,* 23; *herb butter flavoring,* 63; *refrigeration,* 15; *as roasting rack,* 29; *stale and wilted,* 23; *when to add salt,* 64. *See also* names of vegetables
Vermouth-tinged ice cubes, 72
Vinegar-and-oil dressing, 15
Vinegar: *and painted plates,* 15; *uses:* for copper and brass, 103; to get rid of bugs, 23; for cabbage odors, 17; as carpet spot remover, 91; for chocolate cake, 46; for cleaning cookware, 101; for cleaning skillets and teapots, 102; for rinsing crystal, 104; for crisping vegetables, 19, 23; for dishwashing, 99; to set egg whites, 25; for dull floors,

92; to prevent fading of vegetables, 16, 17, 22; for fish odors, 34; for saltwater fish, 34; to remove lime deposits, 98; to tenderize meat, 30; to prevent refrigerator mildew, 97; to reduce sweetness in food, 121; substitute for, 114; to remove white spots on stainless-steel sinks, 98
Vodka, 72

Waffle irons, 103
Waffles. *See* Pancakes and waffles
Wallpapered walls, 94
Walls: *cleaning of,* 94; *gloss for paneling,* 95; *gum erasers for smudges,* 94; *nail holes,* 94–95; *picture paste-ups,* 95
Walnuts, unshelled, 18
Watermelon: *to keep cool,* 76; *testing for ripeness,* 60
Wax (floor), 93
Wax drippings (candles), 66, 68
Whipped cream tips, 54
White kid gloves, 126
Wilted vegetables, 14, 16, 19, 34
Window cleaning, 95
Wine: *cork removal,* 126; *dessert, and flambeing,* 67; *opened, storing of,* 72; *punch making,* 71; *red, and stains,* 67, 128; *for drowning roaches,* 109; *sour, as vinegar substitute,* 114
Wood fires: *igniting damp logs,* 74; *wearing wet gloves,* 75
Woodwork: *cat scratching,* 126; *cold tea cleaning of,* 96; *high gloss for,* 95; *filling in holes,* 95
Worms and plants, 110
Wrinkling: *of baked apples,* 56; *of buns,* 43

Yeast, 43
Yeast breads, 42–43

SHARE YOUR FAVORITE HINTS WITH US.

Send to:

MARY ELLEN'S BEST OF HELPFUL KITCHEN HINTS
1605 West Lake Street
Minneapolis, Minn. 55408

No purchase is necessary to qualify.
Simply send in your original hints.
If they are used in forthcoming sequels of
Mary Ellen's Best of Helpful Kitchen Hints
you will be notified and sent a free copy
of our next great book of helpful hints.

Submission of Best Hints by readers
constitutes your permission for accepted hints
to be published in any sequels.

NOW THERE ARE TWO...

MARY ELLEN'S BEST OF HELPFUL HINTS
and
MARY ELLEN'S BEST OF HELPFUL KITCHEN HINTS

First there was MARY ELLEN'S BEST OF HELPFUL HINTS—the one indispensable book for every household. Hints for every room in your home; hints on beauty, cleaning, painting, laundry, pets, gardening, storage, sewing...and much, much more!

spiral-bound paperback $4.50

Now there is also MARY ELLEN'S BEST OF HELPFUL KITCHEN HINTS—no kitchen should be without one. Hints on cooking, baking, entertaining, barbecues, freezing, cleaning, trash, making do...and much, much more!

spiral-bound paperback $4.50

AND NOW THERE IS A SPECIAL EDITION OF THE ORIGINAL HELPFUL HINTS FOR EVERY GIFT OCCASION

A special hardcover edition of MARY ELLEN'S BEST OF HELPFUL HINTS—designed for constant use, a durable red cover makes this book an ideal gift for yourself and all your friends.

special hardcover gift edition $7.95

I would like to order

_____copies of MARY ELLEN'S BEST OF HELPFUL HINTS @ $4.50 each

_____copies of MARY ELLEN'S BEST OF HELPFUL KITCHEN HINTS @ $4.50 each

_____copies of the special gift edition of MARY ELLEN'S BEST OF HELPFUL HINTS @ $7.95 each

Please add 50¢ per order plus 25¢ per copy to your total order to cover postage and handling.
(Please allow 4 to 6 weeks for delivery)

Name_____

Address_____

City_____State_____Zip_____

Mail this page along with your check or money order to:
Warner Books, P.O. Box 690, New York, N.Y. 10019